W9-ADT-722

Death Row Letters

1. Donald Wallace and his family. From left to right: Kathleen Wallace Mason (DW's half-sister); Donald Ray Wallace; Brianna Wallace (Kathleen's daughter); Andrew Mason, Kathleen's husband.

Death Row Letters

Correspondence with
Donald Ray Wallace, Jr.

Charles Leslie

DELAWARE

Newark: University of Delaware Press

© 2008 by Rosemont Publishing & Printing Corp.

All rights reserved. Authorization to photocopy items for internal or personal use, or the internal or personal use of specific clients, is granted by the copyright owner, provided that a base fee of $10.00, plus eight cents per page, per copy is paid directly to the Copyright Clearance Center, 222 Rosewood Drive, Danvers, Massachusetts 01923. [978-0-87413-015-7/08 $10.00 + 8¢ pp, pc.]

Other than as indicated in the foregoing, this book may not be reproduced, in whole or in part, in any form (except as permitted by Sections 107 and 108 of the U.S. Copyright Law, and except for brief quotes appearing in reviews in the public press).

Associated University Presses
2010 Eastpark Boulevard
Cranbury, NJ 08512

The paper used in this publication meets the requirements of the American National Standard for Permanence of Paper for Printed Library Materials Z39.48-1984.

Library of Congress Cataloging-in-Publication Data

Leslie, Charles M., 1923–
 Death row letters : correspondence with Donald Ray Wallace, Jr. / Charles Leslie.
   p. cm.
 Includes bibliographical references.
 ISBN 978-0-87413-015-7 (alk. paper)
 1. Wallace, Donald Ray—Correspondence. 2. Leslie, Charles M., 1923—
Correspondence. 3. Death row inmates—Indiana—Correspondence. 4. Death
row—Indiana. I. Wallace, Donald Ray. II. Title.
HV8699.U5L46 2008
364.66092—dc22   2007032359

PRINTED IN THE UNITED STATES OF AMERICA

Contents

Preface

THOUSANDS OF MEN AND WOMEN ARE NOW ON DEATH ROW IN American prisons. Some of them have been convicted for crimes they did not commit. Opponents of capital punishment emphasize this fact, and it is widely publicized when a death row prisoner is exonerated. But what about the guilty? The correspondence in this book is with Donald Wallace, a thief and murderer executed by the State of Indiana on March 10, 2005.

According to David Dow, a law professor who has defended death row prisoners for many years, "Most capital murder defendants have committed the crime the state has accused them of committing." He describes them as a group in this manner, "If you show me a death row inmate, I will tell you his biography. People on death row are poor. They were abused as children, emotionally or physically. They are uneducated. They came from homes so dizzyingly broken that describing them with the word dysfunctional is not even remotely adequate. They grew up abusing alcohol, drugs, or people. . . . On death row, almost all of them—not every one of them, but most—exhibit the entire range of characteristics that make a person human. They grow up in homes and neighborhoods where their humanity is quashed and assaulted, but they routinely heal on death row." [1]

Donald Wallace exactly fits this profile. His victims were Patrick and Theresa Gilligan, both 30 years old, and their children, Lisa, who was 5, and 4-year-old Gregory. The family lived in a middle class neighborhood of Evansville, Indiana.

The present book records correspondence with Wallace over the last five years of his life. His first letter describes the murders. Observing his skill as a writer, I asked whether he might construct other narratives of the crime, citing *Rashomon*, a Japanese film that famously gives conflicting first-hand accounts of a murder. Though I discussed it with him during a visit to the prison, Wallace rejected the sugges-

---

1. David R. Dow, *Executed on a Technicality: Lethal Injustice on America's Death Row* (Beacon Press: Boston, 2005), pp 5 and 186.

tion. I did not think his account was false. Still, reality often has dimensions that cannot be reduced to a single narrative. Evidence that DW's story could have been told differently appears in several places in our correspondence. The point for him would remain the same, that he was responsible for his crime. He did not want me to research his case, or to contact anyone in his family. He wanted me to accept him for what he appeared to be in letters and during our visits.

Since Wallace was an autodidact and I was a college professor I assumed that I could help with his education. Instead, as our correspondence developed, I served as a foil for his intellectual aspirations while he acted as my instructor. Our letters record a relationship between two people as different as night and day set in the landscape of American crime and punishment. We disagreed about fundamental issues of science, philosophy, and religion, but it helped that we both held skeptical views of current events, including two presidential elections, the political exploitation by the Bush administration of the 9/11 terrorist attacks, and the Iraq war.

This book is an epistolary narrative in which Donald Wallace should have the final word by way of introduction. The following letter, written four months before his execution, is from a series of autobiographical letters to Maureen Hayden, a journalist at the *Evansville Courier*. Hayden's interpretation of those letters will be discussed in the postscript to this volume. I have selected one to satisfy manuscript readers who wanted me to provide a sociological description of the Indiana death row. Wallace, having lived on death row for many years, gives an insider's description of the community created by prisoners themselves. He begins with the view from the tiny window of his cell. He could not have seen details of the pastoral scene that he describes. He was imagining a joyous *Peaceable Kingdom*, "a world full of miracles," to frame his analysis of the setting in which those sentenced to death for unforgivable crimes may nevertheless find redemption. It is an idealized description of an evolving social system, but people on death row throughout the United States often change deeply, seeking to better themselves. He recalls men he admired who became his friends before they were executed, one African-American in particular. The community was shattered when, fifteen months before he wrote this letter, death row was transferred to a supermax prison in which inmates were radically isolated from each other. Wallace joined sixteen other prisoners in a hunger strike to protest their new circumstances. The story of that strike is recorded in the present volume.

November 18, 2004

Dear Maureen,

It's early in the morning. I sit at the end of my bunk, writing on a little stainless steel "table"—a shelf attached to the wall actually. Directly before me is a narrow window, a vertical slit 5″ wide by 36″ tall and 10″ deep. Because it is so deep, the field of view is narrow. But it widens with distance and I can see the cars passing east and west along Hwy 6 some 1,500 yards in the distance—across a farmer's field (wheat this year, corn last year) and past a nearer sewage treatment complex. There are three oak trees nearby, and this is the third time I'll see them naked and skeletal in the dead of winter soon to come. They were bare when I got here in February of 2003. I watched spring magically resurrect them; watching them surge under the summer sun . . . only to wither and yellow and bare themselves to another season of death. But then comes all the joy of spring again, and dandelions burst forth like fireworks, and summer makes everything green and vibrant again. And there is a parade of animals that dance to this silent waltz: squirrels, woodchucks, skunks, raccoons . . . and year round Canada Geese parade past the double fence (oblivious to its angry snarls of razor wire) with their little fluffy brown chicks in tow. And slowly they grow and fledge and look like carbon copies of their sires and dams. And I sigh. How did I not see all of this? A world full of miracles in every direction, a treasure-house for anyone who stops and looks. Somehow I got caught up into an ever-escalating cycle of emotional reaction that blinded me to everything not part of my own projections. And I try to remember who that angry and confused kid was, try to recall what he was thinking. . . . But he is alien to me now—almost incomprehensible.

So I wrote all of that to preface an answer to your question about death row culture. It's difficult to answer because it isn't static at all, but is constantly evolving. When I first came to death row there were only 12 of us there. The death penalty had only recently been restored, so no one was close to death unless they volunteered like Steven Judy had, and like a few others would later. Only one of us was past his 20s. Seventy-five percent of us had done time before in the era when the "convict code" prevailed. So we spent time educating the other twenty-five percent on how to "sail," all the do's and don'ts of the "Stand-up Convict." But most of us, certainly I, were in a state of arrested development. I mean by this that we'd had lives of trouble and reaction that stopped us from integration either within ourselves or within society as a whole. So we occasionally squabbled and had petty tiffs. But the convict code dealt with all of that. We had many who were above average in intellect, too: Ziyon Ben-Ysrayl (Tommie Smith), JR Thompson, Larry Williams, Asamu Nassor (Greg Resnover), to name a few. For the first five years or so we grew up together, adding new people like Marv Bieghler, Mark Wisehart, Kevin Conner, Stu Kennedy, and others.

Someone like Phillip Zimbardo would have loved to watch all of this unfold. It would be a social psychologist's dream. We established equilibrium, and then someone new would show up—an independent variable that changed the whole equation. But we had a good core group of strong and intelligent leaders who were active in keeping things on an even keel. We had enough to worry about with our cases and oppressive prison conditions, let's not add to it ourselves. This is more difficult to do when the numbers of prisoners increase. But we were fortunate to have established an order that prevailed because it made natural sense.

All of this led to a camaraderie like nowhere else in prison. On the main line of prison there are all kinds of divisions, some very sharply defined, that keep prisoners tense against each other. Race, gangs, city of origin, and a dozen other lesser factors divide prisoners against themselves. But we got past all of these on death row. Only race had to be revisited occasionally.

Racism is simply a part of American life. I know we're trained to evade this truth through p.c. politics and slogans, but the fact is that race issues eat at the underbelly of our culture. On the streets you segregate from each other and have enough lebensraum, as it were, to pretend that everything is peachy between you. But it's not. On death row we were confined in close quarters with each other. So we had to visit the issue of race and racism again and again. And the more you roll up your sleeves and shovel at the pile of dung the more you see that the problem is deeper, more pervasive, and more subtle than you ever imagined. So slowly each side began to see each other better, and to work through the hard spots. But mostly we acknowledged that we were all too conditioned by life to eliminate it, and that we'd have to work through things again and again.

When you live with the same people 24 and 7, for years and years, you get to know them intimately. No strength or weakness remains hidden in this crucible, and all your slag floats to the top. In the end you begin to see how much every human being is more alike his fellows than he is different from them. Once you skim off that slag, the basic metal is the same. So this crucible tends to purify you.

It is ironic that regular prison, the place that is supposed to "correct" you, only makes you worse. Everything in it is like the lines from Wilde's "The Ballad of Reading Gaol":

> The foulest deeds from blackened seeds
> Grow well in prison air;
> It's only what is good in man
> That wastes and withers there.

But death row is more like that Quaker ideal from which we get our word "penitentiary"—a place for penitent reflection. Death Row, where we are supposed to rot as the unredeemable condemned, actually promotes redemption in ways ordinary prison cannot. So when we were kids we talked like prisoners about heroic amatory and criminal adventures. But within 5 years most of us were sincerely asking what—in a world of relative values with no absolutes—is good and true? Many of us began to study philosophy and religion and psychology in a search for values that were true and good. Okay—they're going to kill me, and treat me like shit until they do. But just for me, let me be a better human being when I die.

Some get worse. Some are mentally unsound and unable to improve. But it would surprise you how ubiquitous is this self-purifying desire on death row. Ziyon Ben-Ysrayl's transformation was amazing. I met him on lock-up in Pendleton in the 70s, when he was Tommie Smith. His nickname was "Priest," taken from his mother's name, "DuPriest." He was hardcore, street tough, an unabashed criminal. But he followed the convict code, so you could trust him not to backstab you. But he was hardcore. When I met him again on death row we reminisced about Pendleton, all the crazy things we'd done and seen there. We were not much different than before. Priest was always intelligent. We'd play chess and talk idle chit-chat, which led to talk about the way the world was, and so forth. We were on parallel tracks to the same questions, so we often exchanged books. Then we'd discuss them. And others would join in. The cells were all open-faced— just bars in the front—so everyone could converse while in their cells. Some nights the whole block would engage in all-night discussions. Priest became quieter and more reflective for awhile. Then he became a Hebrew Israelite, a Messianic branch of Judaism that accepts the New Testament. He changed his name to Ziyon Ishua Ben-Ysrayel.

And he poured himself into his faith and into study. I've never seen anyone change so much. At the end he was a bona fide holy man. You could see it in his eyes, you could feel sacred power radiating from him. He lay on the execution table for one hour and thirty-five minutes while they fumbled to find his veins, poking him full of holes, finally slicing open his foot to sew in the catheter. And through all of this he was serene, with his God. The warden, Al Parke, at one point had to leave the room to wipe his face and gather himself. I respect Al Parke a lot for that glimpse of his humanity in an inhumane situation.

Funny, isn't it? You sentence a guy to death because he seems to be unredeemable, but you end up killing a guy who has become a redeemer to others. Sometimes our way of looking at things is like a dog chasing its own tail. He never catches it, but often bites himself in the ass.

Well . . . I hope I've done justice to the question that was difficult to frame. I could tell you the mindless details, but this is the real bread. I can't articulate the whole of it because it evolves through years of small moments and little realizations. But I've done what I could.

Peace and Blessings
DW

Death Row Letters

I
The Year 2000

1

Becoming Acquainted

May 17, 2000

Dear Mr. Wallace,

Last week I got the enclosed application form to visit you from Tom Miller, who got it in turn from the prisoner he visits, Kevin Conner. Miller and I attend the local Quaker Meeting.

My wife and I moved to a retirement community in Bloomington last year. I was a Professor of Anthropology at the University of Delaware. I have an unpaid appointment as an Adjunct Professor at Indiana University.

I grew up in southern Arkansas. During World War II I earned my wings as a B-17 pilot in the Army Air Corps. After the war I went to the University of Chicago on the G.I. Bill and soon married a girl who worked as a secretary in the Dean's office. We have three children and four grandchildren. I am 76 years old.

My field research was a summer with the Fox Indians in Iowa and a year in a Zapotec town in southern Mexico for my doctoral thesis. From 1961 on, my research was in India on indigenous systems of medicine.

I will have surgery on my back on May 25. Recovery will take a few weeks. If you are interested in my visiting you, I could do it during the first week of July. Would July 5 be possible? Or July 6 ?

Sincerely,
Charles

May 21, 2000

Dear Charles,

Hi, and thanks for your letter. Kevin Conner had told me to expect to hear from someone in the near future. That's sort of like a blind date, and you never know what you're getting when you agree to that kind of contact. So I was pleasantly surprised to discover that you are intelligent, educated, and can probably carry on a decent conversation. I like your profession as well. Having had 20 years on death row to figure out who I am and what I like most in life, I figure I'd do best in the free world as either a perpetual college student or a monk. Or perhaps both.

I'm 42 years old. I was 22 and just coming out of prison when my crime occurred. Four counts of murder.

I didn't get off to a very good start in life. I was blessed with the native gifts of intelligence, passable looks, and athleticism. But things started going badly at four when my parents were divorced. I spent a lot of effort in trying to get them back together. This entailed attempts to sabotage any new relationships they found. Unless I'm cursed with contrary genes and therefore all of this would have happened anyway, I can trace that time as the beginning of a treaty of reciprocal violence with the world. Being bent on sabotage, I was an unruly child. Since my childish plans never seemed to work, I became frustrated. But also I was a pain in the ass to all, and pretty soon I was feeling acute rejection from both parents. From those humble beginnings, affairs progressed to their present state.

Always in trouble at school. Fighting, skipping, lying, stealing. Started taking drugs at 11. Got into the hippie culture of those times—most likely because their spirit of rebellion matched mine. I finally got expelled from school halfway through the eighth grade. I never attended school again after that except part of a semester as a high school freshman when I got out of reform school a few years later. Indiana law says you have to be in school until you're 16. So, at just the moment when I was congratulating myself for a job well done in getting kicked out, I was informed that I had to go to an institution called Father Gilbault's School for Boys in Terre Haute, Indiana.

It wasn't a bad place, really. But I had run away from home several times and survived it well. I considered myself a little man, able to govern his own life. So I escaped from Gilbault's any chance I got.

There's probably nothing worse for a kid than to have absolute freedom. To be able to do whatever you want, whenever you want, however you want. But that's what being on the road as an escapee is like. From my point of view, it was great. I traveled the proverbial highways and biways of the nation. Visited most of our big cities. I was a clever boy, and I figured out survival skills that the other runaway kids I met hadn't thought of at that time. (Most of them are condemned either to petty crime or to selling sexual favors to pedophiles. I had different ideas.) I became a general purpose felon, usually taking the path of least resistance leading to the most gain. It worked pretty well. I learned great job skills for a criminal. An older woman (she was 17) taught me how to run interference for her as she picked pockets. She was very good. All I had to do was bump into someone and arrest their progress, and then throw a fit of "watch where you're going, asshole!" profanity in their face so as to wholly distract them. Carol would lift their goods as clean as you please.

So my developmental years—when most kids are learning to do their homework and "honesty is the best policy"—I was learning that one survived by whatever means were necessary. They were neither good nor bad; all acts were judged according to their effectiveness.

By now you may be thinking you got the wrong draw on the "blind date" aforementioned. But let me say this. In spite of all I was doing then, there was no real malice in my heart. I took no glee in what I did or refrained from doing. As a kid I was barred from ordinary employment. And I learned the lesson any lad quickly gleans in a society such as ours: money talks, and bullshit walks. When you bring cash, no one asks too many questions. In any case, despite my one-boy crime wave, it was all happy go lucky with me. A lark.

Street kids are strange. If they stay at it for awhile, there's a peculiar cast to their eyes. Ancient wisdom shining from the eyes of children. You learn a lot on the streets. It makes you tougher, warier, quicker, and more instinctive in your approach to life. But then they capture you and try to treat you like a child again.

Filled with the hubris of youth, though, you are contemptuous of such treatment. You are fairly certain that you could survive— thrive—in scenarios in which they'd perish. They seem like children to you. You can't go back. Lost innocence is lost forever. You can't un-know what you've learned. So you rebel at this attempt to treat you as an ordinary child again. For whatever reason, I still had this "You started it!" mentality that kids on the playground believe is perfect jus-tification. I hadn't done anything wrong in my mind. So why am I being punished?

Anyway, when reform school finally granted me a parole, neither of my parents would take me into their homes. Ouch! Not that I didn't deserve it, I suppose. But still, that cut pretty deeply. It also seemed to verify the suspicion I'd long harbored that they never loved me to begin with. They both had new families and were doing well. I was the last thing they needed in their lives. So they cut their losses and bet on their new families.

I'm not a psychologist. I can't tell you when pain metamorphoses into resentment and malice. But somewhere along the line it began to happen to me. The most striking thing to me now is how shallow my existence became. I didn't have a clue as to who I was, or what values I held. In the gulf of that ignorance I began to do the only thing I knew how to do. I created a persona: bits from here and there. Whatever struck me as cool. I wrapped it around me like a cloak and told the world, "Here I am. This is me." But I didn't know who I was or what I wanted. I was lost. I faked it pretty well, nevertheless. The show must go on, right?

Things went on like that. The past was painful; the future was barren. So I lived like the steely in a pinball machine, bouncing from the bumper of one event to another, careening all over the place. A sense of hopelessness overcame me. I fought it off with drugs. Heroin and its opiate relatives, speed, hallucinogens, whatever the situation called for. Drugs became the point of my existence. Since they are expensive, I resorted to the skills I'd learned so well as a younger boy. At 17 I was sent to a maximum security prison—the Indiana Reformatory at Pendleton. That was in June of 1975. At that time they called Pendleton a "Gladiator School" because it was mostly filled with young prisoners who wanted to make a convict name for themselves. Believe me, at 17 you had to be tough to survive this and keep your dignity and rectum intact. I was pretty tough, having endured many adventures in early life. Reform school had taught me how to hold my own. But prison was the Major Leagues. So I made this decision. I decided that I would be prepared at every instant to kill or die in defense of my person and property. I began to chant a sort of mantra in my mind: "Don't think. Don't try to talk your way out of it. When a threat comes, strike hard and strike fast, and don't stop until you win through or die." It's a terrible thing. But I felt like my entire sense of self was at stake. So I chanted that mantra.

If you chant a mantra long enough it begins to chant itself through you. I was tested: cut one prisoner's throat from ear to ear in the first month I was there. Two months later I stabbed another prisoner. Both brought it to me, I didn't initiate the conflict. ("He started it!" I guess was the playground mentality again.) In one more incident I cracked a prisoner's head with a steel pipe. After that no one really bothered me. Ah! But that mantra rattled around in my skull like dice in a Backgammon cup. I couldn't turn it off. I lived for two years like a coiled spring. I walked wide around corners, and entered every room assessing all threats and what furnishings could be turned to my advantage in the event of trouble. It's a terrible existence when I look at it now, but at the time it seemed merely to be the way things were. No more, no less. Then they let me out. At 19 I was reformed.

Walking around the streets the mantra was still ticking off its count like the clock on a bomb. Through the filter of what I had become, I couldn't see this. Everything seemed "normal" to me. But friends began to avoid me. People were afraid of me. I could go from 0 to 120 mph in terms of temper in a second. I looked to the future and couldn't see myself in it. I can't tell you the despair that comes from looking into nothingness. I relied on my old familiar friends, drugs, and crime to pay for them. I had no job skills, and I had no work habits. I was trained in crime, and I knew its ways.

From my present vantage I was shallow beyond belief. My personality was a work in progress, I repeated cool-sounding lines from books and movies. I reacted to events the way I imagined the characters I drew my "identity" from would act in that situation. I knew what I was doing. The despair in this was even more terrible than the knowledge of having no future. I hadn't even a present. I suppressed this with whatever drugs I could find and finally got busted again.

Back in prison at 20 no one messed with me. The mantra had a life of its own now. Threat/Strike. Threat/Strike. It was reflexive now, and reinforced by being submersed again in the crucible in which it was first smelted for casting. Then they let me out again.

Same routine: drugs and crime. My girlfriends always were strippers or prostitutes. Beautiful, but damaged goods like me. I'm not sure under which rubric that properly falls: "misery loves company" or "birds of a feather." Not sure if I ever loved any of them, but I thought I did. After five weeks out I got busted for burglaries and possession of stolen goods and got out on bond.

I decided to leave town. My uncle lived in Houston, Texas, and he said he could get me a job starting at $7.50 an hour in the factory where he worked. Houston was in a boom then, and workers were wanted. I thought I might as well try that. Maybe there was some future. Maybe I'd find it in Houston. But I needed cash to get there. Just one more burglary, then, and I'd be off to a brighter tomorrow.

Never get a house with deadbolt locks that take a key from both sides. They're a mild annoyance to burglars who want in, but once in they trap you inside. The family whose house I was burglarizing returned home through the only open door. Threat/Strike. I went on autopilot. It was almost like watching a horror film that some maniac had written. It seemed like I was merely a spectator as my preprogrammed routines took over. I shot them all. Don't think. Don't try to talk your way out. Just strike fast and hard, and don't stop until you win through or die. And then I was standing there dumbly surveying what I had done. Gun smoke hung in the air like the smoke from an unattended cigarette in a quiet room. Some routines were still clicking away, performing evidence cleaning in a haphazard way. And this terrible feeling welled up within me. All the pain I'd ever felt burst in from everywhere at once. I wanted to cry or howl. I wanted to jump out of my skin. What psyche I had shattered like a broken mirror, and here were its pieces lying dead on the floor before me. I fled. What else could I do?

It wasn't long before I was caught.

I went through the trial numbly. I was caught up in something beyond me. There was nothing to do but sit there. Have you ever read Camus' *The Stranger*? I felt like the protagonist felt at his murder trial. My life was a lot like his.

After two years and 10 months awaiting trial I was brought to death row. I was different, but still fishing about for identity. It took about ten years before I could really begin to face my life. When you spend enough time in a cell you are finally forced to confront yourself. How did all this happen? How did I come to be here? At first you feel sorry for yourself. You begin to realize all the potential you had and threw away for nothing. You look around for someone to blame. Hoping at least for the solace of it not being your fault. Some guys gravitate to that theme and stick to it with vigor. But I couldn't. Even those who injured me were injured themselves. I began to think of all the people I'd known and the ways in which I'd hurt them. I began to realize that I was like the prince from the Arabian Nights who, having asked the djinn to bring him his worst enemy's head in a box opened it to find himself staring up at his suddenly headless torso. I was the author of all my woes. I still didn't know quite what to do about any of it.

I began to study textbook materials on philosophy, math, and the sciences. I had always known that I was smart, but now I realized how ignorant I was in spite of that. The more I learned, the more painfully aware of that ignorance I became. As part of my philosophical studies I began also a study of comparative religion.

Seemed like every sect had a fragment of truth in its hands. Once you get past the fabled aspects and begin to understand the true nature of myth you see that there are truths in these things. I began to build a syncretic system of practices: hatha yoga, meditation, concentration exercises. No dogma, just a systematic search. If there was truth in these things, I would find it. If not, I'd know to look elsewhere.

While doing this I taught myself to read and write Latin. As part of my research into Qabalah I learned all the Hebrew and Greek letters and their numerical values to use in a sort of numerological aspect of that system. Recently I decided to learn Greek. I'm still working on that.

I've learned a great deal since I came here. Being only 22 when I was locked up, I've been locked up now almost as long as I was alive before the crime. I don't know if I can ever forgive myself for what I did. Not only for killing four people, but for all the hurt I caused others in my life. Maybe there are some things that cannot or should not be forgiven. I don't know. I do the best I can. Is there any life so ruined that it can't be redeemed? I don't know. But I believe one should try with all one's heart to be better today than he was yesterday. The past I can't change. But I have found out who I am and what I want. No more pretending. After all, one has to do one's homework, and honesty is the best policy.

That's the short story of my life—my confession, if you like. I wish it were prettier, but "the hand of history, having writ, moves on." And no tears nor wishes nor regrets will call it back again. I think they will kill me soon. But then, we're all under a sentence of death. The question is, what about today? For me the answer is doing better than I did yesterday.

I don't know if you got more or less than you expected as a reply. I'd rather put everything on the table up front. The prison has to approve you to be on my visiting list, but this probably won't take long. I wasn't planning on doing anything important on July 5th or 6th, so come on up if you want to.

Until next time,
Don

June 6, 2000

Dear Donald,

Your letter arrived just as I was leaving home for surgery in India-napolis. Our daughter, who works in the Arizona Department of Public Health, read it aloud in the car while I drove.

I may visit the prison with Tom Miller on June 17th. Tom offered to show me the way. It is a long trip, and at first I wasn't sure that I could do it, but I can make the trip. The back surgery was a major operation, but the aftermath has been easier than expected.

Your life story is shocking. Your ability to write it the way you have in this letter is admirable. At the moment I am listening to blues music that reminds me of performers Alan Lomax recorded in Southern prisons years ago. That music transforms raw suffering. As a writer you also transform the experiences of a bad life. Of course, there are many ways to tell a story. Have you heard of the Japanese movie called *Rashomon*? It is the story of a young knight and a beautiful young woman (his bride or betrothed?). They are on horses and he is leading her through a forest when they are set upon by a robber who kills the knight. A peasant woodsman hidden in the bushes observed the whole thing. The story is retold in separate episodes by the peasant, the robber, the bride, and by the dead knight speaking through the medium of a shaman possessed by his spirit. Each story is radically different. "The Rashomon effect" is the disconcerting consequence of recounting the same events from different perspectives.

My productive life essentially ended ten years ago when I retired. It seemed that my life was over because I had invested so much in my work. I was puzzled that the ending was better that I ever expected and wondered how to make a story of it. I tried to remember events in detail, but I could not. How can you explain a life you can't even remember? I could recall only a rough outline of my childhood. I didn't remember the names of playmates, of adolescent friends, or the names of guys I flew with while a cadet in the Army Air Corps. This gave me a new respect for people who write whole books about their childhood, or adolescent coming of age. So many possible stories over a life span, but trying to recall them I realized that I never knew much about most of the people I have known, even my parents. To construct narratives I would have to guess what people were like. Finally, I realized that there wasn't a single life story, and that any of the stories I might tell could be told in different ways. This is the issue in *Rasho-mon*. A fashionable academic term is "decentered." To decenter someone is to get him to doubt his own conviction about himself, or things he believes to be true. Your narrative of a life in crime is organized to explain how you came to kill four people when caught in the midst of a robbery. It is persuasive. It adds up. It is centered, but I wonder whether there are things that this story does not account for. As in most lives, your story could be told differently.

I appreciated your letter, and so did my wife and daughter.

Sincerely,
Charles Leslie

June 25, 2000

Dear DW,

If I seemed dumb when we met on Saturday it was partly because I have trouble separating background noise from conversation. The hallway clatter was deafening for me. When I moved closer to you and watched your lips I understood pretty well, but when Kevin and Tom joined in I missed most of what was being said.

I could not rise to the level of intellectual exchange you wanted to engage in. I understood that you have read a lot about religion, have a sophisticated conception of life as a gift, and do not believe in life after death, or in divine intervention in human affairs. Emily Dickenson wrote, "Of course I prayed, and did God care? He cared as much as on the air a bird had stamped her foot and cried, 'Give me!'"

Anyway, it was good to meet you. You may think of some way that I could be useful to you. If you do, let me know. Opposition to the death penalty is currently a major issue in Illinois and Indiana. It should be an issue in the presidential race this year. There were 131 executions while Bush was Governor of Texas. Unfortunately, Al Gore hasn't gotten the message.

I can buy books for you if there is something you particularly want.

We will drive to La Porte to visit friends on July 5, and visit you the next morning. I will stay only an hour because we will drive on to a vacation house we have rented in northern Michigan.

Sincerely,
Charles

June 30, 2000

Dear Charles,

I received your letter today, for which thanks. I enjoyed meeting you and look forward to our next visit. I picked up on the fact that you couldn't hear well. My hearing isn't as good as it used to be. I can't imagine how it would be if I lived until I was 76. I found your conversation to be lively and entertaining. I wasn't looking for some jaunt into the abstruse realms of nonsense that many intellectuals seem to desire. So you didn't disappoint me there.

I would very much like to read your books. The only books on my wish list are a good classical Greek-English lexicon, and a good Latin-English dictionary, and *The Egyptian Book of the Dead* by A. E. Wallis Budge. Maybe you could find well-worn used copies for a cheap price at IU. Otherwise, anything and everything interests me. Are you able to use an Indiana University mailing label? I doubt they'll take it on faith here if it's a handwritten return address.

I'm enclosing a drawing I did the other day. Call it "Dream Girl of Castaway Island." That's where I'd like to be, with her and a cargo of books jettisoned from a ship in rough seas and washed up on shore where you can laze in the sun all day and watch shooting stars all night. Moreover, look at the ass on that lass!

I also didn't tell you that I'm a guitarist. I have a guitar here. Sometimes I play as much as ten hours a day. I've become very good. I used to be into only blues and rock 'n' roll, but later I discovered classical music, Spanish classical, jazz, folk, and anything else I can lay an ear to. I'm a far better guitarist than I am an artist. I can't get a tape recorder, else I'd make you a tape. What I play goes into the air and disappears forever.

> Until next time,
> DW

July 16, 2000

Dear Charles,

I enjoyed our visit. Too bad it was so short. I enjoyed hearing about your travels and the things you've seen.

2. *Dream Girl of Castaway Island.*

A couple of things about our visit proved that my previous narrative was atypical for its tightness. I meant to ask you about your foot injury.

I haven't read the whole book of essays on Asian medicine you sent me. Your chapter was interesting to me for more reasons than you might expect. For one, I've been a student of the Western Occult Tradition for quite some time. It is entirely syncretic, mixing bits and pieces from nearly everywhere in an attempt to build a cohesive and exhaustive system. Most often it fails to be either. Some of the nomenclature of Ayurveda is in that mix. But the terms are put forth in whispers, as if they revealed profound occult secrets. You wouldn't believe, for example, the freighting of the three guna: rajas, tamas, and satvas. They are said to represent everything from radiation, conduction, and convection to peace, activity, and sloth; to Sphinx, Hermanubis, and Typhon, and about seven million things in between. Perhaps people esteem things merely because they are foreign and exotic seeming. I probably found your chapter interesting for reasons that you didn't intend.

I notice that you mentioned skepticism in your chapter of the book. Are you a pure skeptic? I try to be, but sometimes I think there are places for skepticism and other places where it is useless. Wittgenstein drew an analogy between the way we use language and the way we play games, saying that both have rules and moves that make sense only in the context of a particular game. He used this analogy to point out that philosophers often make moves in one context that only make sense in another, as when they try to verify religious statements as if they were a part of science. Do you buy that analogy?

I'm also sometimes enamored of William James's "will to believe." He held that in the absence of decisive evidence the mind may create belief in order to act, often resulting in discovery. He even held that belief in such situations was a human right not to be shied from. Have you ever read James? What do you think of his notion? Sometimes I'm skeptical, like when I'm writing a formal piece for thinking people. But I have this wild streak in me that echoes Kant's thesis, that "happiness is not an ideal of reason, but of imagination." I love David Hume and Bertram Russell, both skeptics. But there's another type of skepticism that seems like nothing more than the fear of being duped. I don't like that kind. I'd rather be a fool who took a chance than a pillar of disbelief firmly planted in one safe place.

To completely change the subject. I wanted to ask, are B-17s hard to fly? My uncle used to own a Beechcraft Sundowner, a low-wing single engine plane. My father had a pilot's license, and I used to fly with both of them. It was easy for me to learn the principles of flight, and the feel of flying the plane came quickly to me, although I never landed, which is where skill comes into play. Were B-17s easy or hard to fly? Did you enjoy flying? Did you ever use your piloting skills later in life?

It seems to me that your wife has been the love of your life. You mention her as being with you in your travels. Was she also a fellow scholar in the formal sense of the word?

Enough for today. I have two more letters to write.

> Until next time,
> DW

July 23, 2000

Dear DW,

Thanks for the letter. I enjoyed our visit but didn't want to make my wife wait too long. The waiting room is not attractive, as you can imagine.

Let me respond to your questions.

My foot. In 1965 I was in Calcutta organizing what was to be a six-month research stay. It was June, the beginning of the monsoon season, and I was in the neighborhood of the medical school waiting at a corner for a streetcar. The common practice was to mount the steps of the car while it was still moving. One came along and slowed slightly at the corner. I grabbed the bar next to the door, but then it sped up, so I trotted beside it. It was faster than I could run, so I fell. The next thing I knew I was sitting in the street with my right foot looking like an anatomical drawing. This is called a "degloving accident." The most common occurrence is when someone wearing gloves is working on a machine and a glove gets yanked off taking skin from the fingers with it. One surgeon told me that he once saw a degloved penis.

Airplanes. Flying a B-17 was like driving a truck. At least that is what I thought at the time. I volunteered in 1943 and spent two months in a College Training Detachment at Kansas State. We were then sent to Santa Ana, California, where we were tested for several weeks. Every day our ranks would thin as men were "washed out." Primary Flight Training was at Dos Palos in the San Fernando Valley.

This was the most fun I had because we flew an open cockpit biwing plane. We wore a helmet and goggles, like in World War I movies. We learned to do loops, spins, and fly upside down. After that we went to Stockton Field and flew twin-engine UCF-78s. Each stage of training was prolonged because the army had enough pilots. When I finally got my wings in early 1945, I had something like 380 hours of solo flying time, much more than earlier cadets would have had. I was then stationed at Kingman, Arizona, as a co-pilot on B-17s. Within a couple of months the war ended in Europe. After flying smaller planes the B-17 seemed very clumsy, but we occasionally entertained ourselves by flying around in the Grand Canyon.

Yes, Zelda and our children have gone with me to the field, but I made some trips alone to India. She was in California with the children when I had the accident that made me a cripple. As the folk song says, she has been "a good ol' wagon," and I hope I have been one, too.

Do you need money to buy typewriter ribbons, paper, or other things? I forgot to ask but assume you have access to a store. Can I send you some money? Do you have any income in prison for these things?

Sincerely,
Charles

August 7, 2000

Dear Charles,

Hi. I got the books last Monday (31 July) on the same day I got your letter. Thanks. Did you know that the Lidell and Scott lexicon you bought for me is pretty much the last word in Greek-English lexicons? I was really surprised to get it. I thought they were inordinately expensive. Anyway, both books are useful. My Latin has been pretty good for awhile, but I needed a good dictionary. I had a token Greek-English lexicon in the back of the Greek grammar book, but now that I have the Lidell and Scott I'm going to be a lot better equipped.

I finally read the whole of *Paths to Asian Medical Knowledge*. It was fascinating. The most interesting thing was that now I am much better armed against my occultist colleagues who look both ways before whispering some Hindu or Chinese principles, as if they learned them in the Sanctum Santorum itself. Here they were all clearly explained in an anthropological study. So thanks for arming me with all of these profound secrets of the universe! One has to have hobbies in life, and occultism is one of mine.

I can't imagine how eye-bulging an experience it was to have your foot degloved. Was it terribly painful when it happened? Or was it one of those kinds of things where your body, recognizing the nature of the injury, floods you with enough chemicals to make you detached and aloof at the pain? I had my ankle broken so badly one time that it dangled at almost a right angle off my leg. I just said to my friends, very calmly, "get me to the hospital." I've had all the meniscus cartilage removed from my left knee in a series of operations. It hurts pretty steadily, but I still play basketball, and I forget to feel the pain when I'm concentrating on the game. I hope it isn't too bad for you.

Some people are driven through life along the path where their circumstances, desires, and values converge. The point of equilibrium rolls down the road of who they become. Those who get a sense of their own priorities cut straight roads. Others, myself for example, cut dizzying hairpins and switchbacks. So I always wonder how people get on their own road and how straight was that road.

Did you enjoy academia? As you aged around college kids, did they keep you younger at heart? Is it a myth that colleges are full of intellectuals who are far less prone to knee-jerk reactionary antics than regular folk? I tend to like left and liberal causes, but lately I've seen a lot of left-wing extremism emanating from college campuses. It wouldn't be bad if it were only the kids—they're always full of piss and vinegar and spoiling to take on the world—but I wonder about some of the curricula nowadays. Women's Studies and Afrocentric revisionism are two I can think of right off hand. Political correctness. "Semiotics" (speech shapes thought, therefore if we control the speech we reshape thought, or something like that). All men are rapists, dead white Europeans, and their progeny are the villains of the whole world, etc. Does that kind of stuff really rampage across college campuses? For example, having a great deal of experience with Egyptian history, I can annihilate most of the claims of Afrocentrism, including the supposed "fact" that Egyptians and Carthaginians such as Hannibal, were black Africans forever and always. The evidence is ample. I have nothing against black people. I have nothing against them creating their own social mythologies inasmuch as all peoples create myths about themselves. But to put it on a college curriculum and teach it as if it were factual, and under penalty of extreme hostility if you don't toe the party line, is like teaching in college that George Washington really never did tell a lie in his entire life, and the cherry tree story is fact. If you don't believe it we'll send you to sensitivity training. It seems like a disturbing trend. What do you think about these things?

Thanks for the offer of assistance. I can't really receive much in the mail except money, and that has to come via U.S. Postal Money Order. I'm not going to lie; money would make my life easier, if only for saving me from prison food. I can buy bootleg cigarettes, art supplies, guitar strings, and other necessary supplies, but I have three hots and a cot every day. I won't die if I never have another dollar. You, on the other hand, have living expenses. I don't know what your financial situation is. If you have more than enough money (if there is such a thing), then I would welcome any you send. If it cuts into your well-being, then I don't need it that badly. It's enough for me if we can write. I'm an armchair anthropologist, and I enjoy learning about almost anyone I meet.

Yours truly,
DW

August 12, 2000

Dear DW,

Your letter arrived yesterday. I am glad that you like the Greek lexicon. I reread your July 16th letter just now and realize that I did not respond to several things. I was surprised that you connected occult learning with the essays in the book on medical anthropology. When and why did you get interested on occult theories and practices? When I asked about your arm tattoos you explained the Greek lettering, but I forget its meaning. One abstract tattoo, which I thought was symbolic, you said was only decorative. Those were done in prison and looked less professional than the eagle with folded wings. Did they have special meanings for you when you had them done? I expect that everything you decorate your body with is meaningful.

These questions may be too personal.

Your July 16 letter said that I had mentioned being a skeptic in *Paths to Asian Medical Knowledge*. I don't remember that, and am surprised. You bring up Wittgenstein on language games, William James on the "will to believe," quote Kant, and say you like Hume and Bertram

Russell. I should have responded to that. I haven't read philosophy in many years. As an undergraduate in Chicago we got a taste of Aristotle, Plato and other Western philosophers up to Hume, Bentham, and John Stuart Mill. As a graduate student I read Ernst Cassirer and Susan Langer because other social scientists I knew thought that they were great, but the philosophy books I enjoyed were A.N. Whitehead's *Science and the Modern World*, and John Dewey's *Human Nature and Conduct*. I read some William James, and borrowed from him the idea to "pluralize your thought." At least, I often recommended this to students, attributing it to James. I wanted to appear learned, yet I could not have answered any probing questions about James or any other philosopher.

Two good friends when we were at Pomona College were philosophers and much concerned with Wittgenstein. I listened to them, and have heard lectures on his work, but I never studied Wittgenstein. I did read a good biography that related his life to his philosophical development.

So, what can I say? Only that I have been exposed to some philosophy, but make no claims to philosophical knowledge. I suppose that I am a skeptic, but this is more by temperament than from a worked out philosophical position. If I said in the book that I was a skeptic perhaps I was only referring to some of the claims made for Ayurveda by modern practitioners. It wouldn't have occurred to me to declare myself a philosophical skeptic.

One of the philosophers I knew at Pomona, Robert Fogelin (now at Dartmouth) wrote a book on Pyrrhonian skepticism. Pyrrho (360 to 270 BC) was the first great skeptic. He left no writings, though he became court philosopher to Alexander the Great in 334. His ideas are known by what other people wrote about him. Fogelin says that Pyrrhonian skeptics accepted "common beliefs modestly held," and that their philosophy was an "agoge, a way of living." Pyrrho challenged all dogmatic claims, advocating instead "common sense and good judgment in everyday matters." That appeals to me, but I would have called it pragmatism (which adds that a major concern in deciding whether something is true or false is whether or not action based on it works as expected).

Political conservatives trash Enlightenment rationalism: the ideal of using knowledge to improve human affairs. This, of course, is the central purpose of the social sciences. I believe that if anything about human life is divine it is our capacity for critical thinking. Rational insight grounded in experience, along with skepticism about any dogma, is all we have to protect us from disaster. Nevertheless, igno-rance and irrationality are our common lot.

About pain, you are right, if it is not overwhelming you can practice not focusing on it and this makes it tolerable. On the other hand, if pain is intense, then I am for hollering, groaning, or whatever. I did that when the doctors in Calcutta changed the bandages on my foot in the days following the surgery. The head nurse, a Christian tribal from Assam (Hindus and Muslims consider nursing to be a defiling occupation) reprimanded me in a contemptuous manner. I rebuked her in turn for lacking Christian compassion. When the accident oc-curred I was distracted from the pain by the necessity of getting to a hospital in a rickshaw, and by identifying myself when being admitted there. As a consequence I maintained some dignity.

You ask about Political Correctness and Afrocentric theory among academics. I have long acquaintance with diverse institutions, having held faculty appointments at Southern Methodist University, the Uni-versity of Minnesota, and tenure at Pomona College, Case Western Reserve University, New York University, and the University of Dela-ware. I have also been a visiting professor at four other universities. Someone here who spent his whole career at Indiana University com-mented that I obviously couldn't keep a job. The point is that I have firsthand experience of many different schools. I taught through the 1960s, when students were fired up about racial injustices and the Vietnam War. I was at NYU when someone set off a small firebomb in the library of the Bronx campus. No one ever told me or any other teacher I knew personally how to teach our courses.

No doubt about it, our universities have some very foolish profes-sors, and more than a few incompetent ones. There are always prob-lems of maintaining standards. Still, our best universities are among the greatest institutions of learning the world has produced. We also have many first-rate small colleges with extremely talented students and hard working faculties. Even in the second-rate institutions there are always some outstanding faculty and students. Anyone who really wants a good education can get it at our less prestigious schools.

I don't buy the line of critics who assert that universities are con-trolled by politically correct radicals. Our universities and colleges are governed by responsible and rather conservative people who get along with their boards of trustees, composed of the heads of corporations, bankers, lawyers, and other wealthy people. Universities are run by people with elite sentiments whose job is to raise the hundreds of mil-lions of dollars that these institutions require to keep going. There is absolutely no danger that the system of higher education in America will be taken over by socialists, radical blacks, feminists, and homosexuals. It is true that some of these charges come from professors in high prestige schools. That just proves the whole system is an open marketplace of ideas governed by competition in producing knowledge and training students.

Academics are often charged with being small-minded when we are supposed to be generous-minded. I could preach on this theme for a whole night, having had some bad experiences.

Tom and I will drive up to see you and Kevin on August 19th. Meanwhile I bought the enclosed postal money order. You should not hesitate to tell me what you need.

Sincerely,
Charles

August 20, 2000

Dear Charles,

As you can see, this isn't typed on the typewriter I usually use. Mine expired. No way to get it fixed, and there'll be no replacing it with a new one either. They outlawed personal typewriters here a few years back. We could keep the ones we already owned, but when they broke there'd be no repairing or replacing them. So I'll have to borrow old clunkers like this one (a '60s Royal, just like the one I learned to type on with all ten fingers in the early '70s), or I'll relearn to write. I remember how to write, it's just that I write like a deranged 3rd grader, and few can decipher it. In fact, you'd probably have to be an occultist to plumb its archetypal mysteries! Ha! Ha!

I enjoyed our visit yesterday. I don't get many really challenging debates. I think you are indeed a pure skeptic. You also don't play fair. You know too many tricks that someone like me, who's had only half of an eighth grade education, hasn't yet learned to counter in kind. What do I mean?

Arguments ad hominem, for one. I knew that I risked running afoul of the fallacy of "arguing from authority" when I quoted Plato, so I tried to examine an idea of his in light of historical evidence since he wrote *The Republic*. Your argument was, "But Plato was a fascist!" Maybe you meant by that a fascist might spout that same idea. But I judge all statements for themselves, and think that Hitler must have said at least one true thing. When I said, "I have to examine each statement," you interjected peremptorily, "I don't." Moreover, you dismissed the points of several others with accusations like, "He's an anti-Semite!" Most people have at least one ignorant opinion. Many of us are chock full of them. But you can't dismiss every statement of every person who holds at least one idea that you find repugnant. Or can you? This seems inconsistent with the high intelligence you obviously possess.

We didn't have time to discuss your assertion that my "archetypal ideas" came directly from Jung, who "made all that up." You may remember that it was I who complained about the penchant of occultists for grabbing bits and pieces of this or that system to cement the leaks in their overall system of thought, and that mostly they fail. I don't like New Age store-bought occultism. I study the Qabalah. Mythically it was given by God to the angels so that they could transmit it to Man in order that he would have a roadmap to work his way back to the Garden of Eden. The Safed Qabalists formalized the system of "archetypes" some 300 years before Jung was a gleam in his daddy's eyes. Jung stole his archetypes from the Jewish Qabalists. If Joseph Campbell was an anti-Semite, as you say, it seems remarkable to me that he would purloin the product of Jewish thought while at the same time not like that people.

Finally, I do believe in a sort of magical formula whereby self-transformation may be accomplished. You will no doubt scoff. One of the things I couldn't get you away from in your arguments was that occultism was what you viewed it to be, and therefore I had to believe or practice all those things too. But I don't.

The group of associates I confab with has a formal statement on the subject of Magick. They added the Elizabethan "k" both to distinguish it from prestidigitation, and (you'll love this!) change its numerical value. It goes like this:

I. DEFINITION. Magick is the Art and Science of causing change to occur in conformity with will.

II. POSTULATE. Any required change may be effected by the application of the proper kind and degree of force in the proper manner through the proper medium to the proper object.

This statement is ripe for an illustration. Suppose that it is my will to change the Cosmos from one in which Dr. Charles Leslie does not know my occult theses to one in which he is fully informed on them.

I take up my "magical weapons," typewriter and paper; I write the proper "incantations," these sentences in the "magical language" in which Dr. Leslie can understand; I call forth "spirits" to assist my will, such as the guard who picks up mail, and the postal workers, and I constrain them to do my will by conveying my words to you. The postal workers require a "sacrifice" to appease them, and the victim is known as the "first-class postage stamp."

The occultists I hang out with have formalized these things, and the Qabalah is a system, both cataloging and mnemonic, to assist such operations. You can tell me what other occultists believe or practice, but you can't tell me what I believe or practice.

You told me you had gained your information on occultists casually and second-hand. I have spent significant time and effort in quest of the knowledge I've accumulated. Do you suppose I would just toss all that, which I thoroughly enjoy, even if I thought it was all a crock of shit? I think only half of it is a crock of shit. If I thought it was all a crock I'd probably still play the game. Why?

I sit in a cell for 21 hours every day. I have a guitar and a radio. Occasionally I borrow a TV, but I don't really like TV that much. I can draw. I like crossword puzzles and word games and logic and mathematical games. But how many hours a day do you think you can fill with those activities? Try it sometime. Now, oppose all that to this: I like occultists. Most of them. They're generally smart and highly creative. Maybe too creative at times. All ideas can be discussed and picked apart with vigor. How many angels can dance on the head of a pin was the foolish question of the Scholastics. "Who cares?" asks the practical mind, and "Prove there are such things as angels in the first place!" I'll see where the debate goes. That, or I can sit in this cell every day and contemplate the reality that the last thing I'm going to see in this world is the bars that confine me. Take your pick, brother, dwell on the fairytale occult arts or the bars that keep you in a concrete box year after year, month after month, day after day, hour after hour, and ticking second after ticking second.

This is the why and wherefore of my occult hobby. What I believe and what I pretend to believe for the sake of meaning in an otherwise meaningless existence. I can debate it with you, but you should understand my core position first, then you will understand the passion and persistence of my arguments and that I'm not a gullible sot drunk on the pseudo-science of New Age chic.

You ask about my tattoos. Some of them have meaning. Some, like the Eye of Horus, are occult symbols that are partly totemic (identifying with the tribe), and bear some internal meaning derived from the totemic meaning. The spider-web was space filler, but probably also a danger sign for others. Spiders are venomous and not to be trifled with, so there may have been some idea of displaying it totemically as well. The eagle: well, see the works of Jung for eagle symbolism. Also, there are three grim reaper heads, emblems of death, which are probably psychological in nature; some way of coming to terms with a death sentence, or something like that. Anyway, no questions are too personal for me. I am what I am, and my history is my history. I don't love it all, but I don't hide from it either.

I'm glad you were able to disabuse me of the popular media notions that schools of higher learning were beginning to teach feel-good myths in place of truth. One story said there was even a class at a California community college called "Madonna Studies," and the Madonna in question was the pop singer. That seemed preposterous to me, but I had no way of knowing how true or untrue those reports were. Magazines sell more by over-dramatizing things. My window to the world is the media.

Speaking of guitar, you asked what kind of stuff I play. I only played rock 'n' roll 25 years ago. Then I started liking blues and other folk music. Then I chanced upon some of the Bach fugues and canons, which so astounded me that I became interested in classical music. Beethoven, Mozart. Mozart's "Eine Kleine Nachtmusik" sounds like a pop tune almost. I hear it all the time in movies, so it is a popular tune, even if it's not the equivalent of a pop hit. I like his darker stuff, too, like *Requiem*. Don't like opera. Can't get with it. Don't like country music either. That nasal quality raises goose bumps on my skin. What kind of music do you like?

What kinds of things do you do on a given day? I know you still do some writing. Do you work all day? Do you socialize a lot? Do you like the retirement community you moved to? Do you ever go for drives or walks? Or does your foot make you avoid unnecessary walking? Do you ever go swimming, or bowling?

Thanks for the money. It will help. First thing I'm going to do is fill out an order for some new guitar strings.

Yours truly,
DW

2

Hard Wired

Saturday, August 25, 2000

Dear DW,

Your letter arrived Thursday. I owe you an apology for the ad hominem arguments. I was being flip when I said Plato was a fascist, and
meant to be funny while rejecting whatever it was that you attributed
to *The Republic*. I admitted that I had not read that dialogue, and if I
had it would have been so long ago I could not recall any detail. I have
only secondhand knowledge that Plato rejected democratic rule.
When I said that J. Campbell was an anti-Semite, I was just throwing
in this bit of information. It surprised me years ago when I read about
it in the *New York Times* (students protested when Sarah Lawrence,
where he was a professor, accepted money to endow a chair in his
honor). I read *Hero with a Thousand Faces* many years ago, and enjoyed
it, but recall no details.

Your letter made me realize that I failed to communicate my own
sense of ignorance about the things you were talking about. I have
never even looked at a copy of the Qabalah (spelled Cabala in a reference book on my desk, but I recall others using Kabalah). I was interested in what you were saying, and trying to relate it to my
fragmentary knowledge derived from pop culture and brief visits to
bookstores that feature occult literature: thus, my images are of fortune telling with tarot cards, palm readers, astrologists, alchemists,
magicians. All the stuff of New Age mystics concerned with supposedly secret knowledge and ancient wisdom.

When I argued with you I was mainly trying to refute the conception of human nature you started from when you said that "civilization
is a thin veneer," and that our species is "hard wired" to be violent
and aggressive. The great majority of American social scientists are on
the side of nurture in the nature/nurture controversy. You were asserting the nature position by using a currently fashionable computer

39

metaphor, hard wired, which means that behavior is genetically determined. As I understood you, you claimed that natural selection in human evolution favored genes for aggression, and you extended this to other lines of primate evolution as well.

Thousands of years of civilized life represent for you only a "thin veneer" of civil behavior. You claimed that so-called primitive people admire warriors and warriors were favored throughout the historic civilizations (meaning that they would father more children, thus passing more of their genes to following generations than other males, hard wiring the species for violence). You used one bit of evidence that you should abandon right away: canine teeth. Human teeth are very "primitive," meaning in this case, "non-specialized" and thus like the teeth of our early mammal ancestors. Our canines are relatively small, not like those of species that use their mouths to fight and kill. They are the teeth of an animal that evolved with an omnivorous soft diet (insects, seeds, berries, other fruits, fresh twigs, soft parts of animals, like the brain and internal organs, whatever came their way). Perhaps by the mid-Pleistocene, Homo erectus had control of fire, and this allowed cooking that enhanced diet. Tool use with fire allowed greater consumption of meat, favoring male hunting and female gathering. Thus, we became more predatory without the anatomical specializations of other predators through cultural evolution grounded in learned behavior. This narrative has given rise to the notion that we were selected for violence and the kind of territoriality you emphasize. Anthropologists call this "the hunting hypothesis." You made a common additional claim that we are still biologically the aggressive hunter/warrior we were selected to be over the long haul of hominid evolution. Add to this the selection for gender differences: the male an aggressive hunter, the female a nutrient mother who gathers nuts, berries, and insect larva (by most calculations, the bulk of the diet would have been furnished by the females).

While there may be some truth to this evolutionary story, the deduction from it that we are hard wired for aggression and that "civilization is a thin veneer" is very wrong. What you need to do is pluralize your thought. Think of other attributes of our species: the prolongation of infant and childhood dependency to a period of many years; the behavioral flexibility expressed in the adaptation of the species to environmental niches from the arctic to the tropics; language, which moves the species into an imagined world of the past and the future, invites metaphors and analogical reasoning, and leads eventually to writing, so that communication is free of the necessity for face-to-face contact, and knowledge can be stored; the aesthetic character of the species—carving, painting, dancing, poetry, music, jewelry and other body decoration, ritual performance, building homes, temples, pyramids, skyscrapers, cooking foods. Would you say we are "hard wired" for these things, too?

The point is that we are hard wired for extremely varied and complex behavior that requires great flexibility of response, and a high degree of social cooperation. Our emotions of affection, sympathy, loyalty, grief, guilt, shame, etc. are many stranded and woven together by the highly developed capacity to learn that informs our lives from the cradle to the grave. We learn enough to build places as different as New York City, ancient Athens or Ankor Wat, precisely because we are highly socialized animals who cooperate with each other on a large scale over long periods of time. Our highly social nature can be called into play to kill millions of Jews, to create atomic bombs and drop them on Japan, to enslave Africans, and to build things as astonishing as Manhattan, as beautiful as the Taj Mahal, as deeply dedicated to cultivating knowledge as Harvard University or the National Institutes of Health.

So, if you look at the violence and aggression in human conduct, look also at the much more extensive and biologically adaptive behavior based on reason, imagination, and rule abiding sociality. Think of the ordinary meaning of a phrase like "I admire his humanity."

You should assume that we are hard wired to create civilizations, for in fact that is what our species has done. Warriors at any time have been a tiny part of the population, and, of course, there is no evidence that they fathered more children than other men. Probably fewer, since they were more likely to die young.

I have read, or heard, that Jung thought his mental archetypes were genetic. It is simpler to assume that our mentality is shaped by cultural experiences as we grow up in complex societies, learning to respond appropriately to others, and that what we start with is a highly generalized, nonspecific, capacity to experience pleasure, pain, surprise, anger as we learn to get on in the world. The similarities between myths, rituals, and other symbolic systems in different times and places derive from the fact that we are a single species with pair bonding to raise children over prolonged periods of dependency. Thus we have similar experiences, imagine things in similar ways, and reason creatively using analogy and metaphor.

Archaeologists find evidence that the domestication of plants and animals occurred independently at times and in places remote from each other. The most impressive example is the independent invention of the American civilizations, including peasant agriculture, monumental temples, pyramids, metallurgy, precise astronomical observations, writing, the concept of zero, and so on. These things are not hard wired in the human brain; they were invented and reinvented by people over thousands of years.

The evening I returned home from visiting you we watched an hour-long program on public television in which a reporter visited sacred cities on the upper reaches of the Ganges, and then in the company of Indian pilgrims climbed on into the Himalayas until he reached the source of the river in the melting runoff of a glacier. A wonderful touch was an encounter of the filmmaker with a naked sadhu (this one wore a tiny jock strap). He rode a large motorcycle and gave the filmmaker a lift on it to the next town. He had the dreadlocks of a sadhu, and was appropriately on the road, but he also had a transistor radio, spoke good Indian English, and had a pipe to smoke bhang, which made the hitchhiker wonder if it was safe to ride further with him. India will pluralize your thinking in surprising ways.

As the film crew got higher in the mountains, pilgrims were obviously suffering from the cold. Nevertheless, they kept going, and huddled around open fires at night. We were moved by their devotion, their search for the source of the sacred, the desire to be near it, to experience what Indians call darshan. This made me regret having argued with you earlier in the day, recalling your effort to convince me that the possibility of transforming the self was the central motive for your fascination with the Qabalah. I respect that, and was moved by recalling your declaration of belief in spiritual alchemy.

I must stop writing. We leave at 5 a.m. tomorrow to catch a plane to Phoenix to visit our daughter. She leaves in September for three months in India to work in a World Health Organization program to eradicate polio. It has been eradicated from most of the world, but remains endemic in parts of Africa and South Asia.

A final question: I talked to a local lawyer and former member of the Indiana Legislature about the rule that you cannot get a new typewriter nor have yours repaired, or buy a tape recorder. He said I should write the warden, and send a copy to the governor and that he would see that the governor gets it.

Sincerely,
Charles

August 31, 2000

Dear Charles,

Greetings friend. I received your letter yesterday.

I feel like I was either wholly inarticulate in expressing what I thought on our visit, or you were in the midst of an argument with other theories and thought you heard them in my words. Because not only do I not hold with the things you thought I was saying, I would be perplexed if someone said them to me.

First, I say that the good parts of man, by which I mean those that are unlike the animal parts, are hard wired in his neocortex. I accept all of them, and I do not deny or disparage them in any way: art, poetry, theater, charity, temple building, the Taj Mahal. The urge to create civilization is every bit as hard wired in us as is the urge to war. I accept the full range of human potential.

I've never seen a computer. There were no personal computers when I got locked up. When I say hard wired I mean that there is a physical structure composed of neurons, synapses, and so forth that are like wiring. The circuit defines the range of activity within that physical structure. The R [Reticular] complex is the least capable of variety. Part of our instinctive behavior arises from it. The limbic system is more capable of varied expression, and it puts us on a par with most other mammals, including predators. Finally, the neocortex is wonderfully capable of a variety of activity. Before we were even humans the R complex existed. Then the limbic system was grafted onto it, and finally the neocortex was grafted onto the earlier structures. Man is characterized by the activities of the neocortex, but these animal structures still subsist in him. He gives in to instinctive behavior often. The animal parts of him want territory, food, and reproduction. This is not ignoble or bad or evil. It is not destructive or harmful. Any biologist will agree with the statement that every living thing has the instinct to do these things. If you suggest that man dispenses with them, then you suggest that he dispenses with his will to survive.

I do not think man's animal nature is evil in the least, or good. It just is. His higher nature, that complexity originating in the neocortex is what I mean by the "thin veneer." I'm not rehashing someone else's neo-Darwinian argument. I've never read Darwin. I have little interest in genetics. I look at the world and observe certain things about it. I observe that the human has the exact same brain formations as every other mammal, only with an exaggerated neocortex. This makes up the veneer, so I speak from a literal biological standpoint first, and observations second. I only want to know what is. What might be is conjecture. I want to know what is, was and probably will be as a consequence of nature.

I agree with you that racism is bad. But why does it consistently occur among races? If there is no other race around, then men will find some other difference to distinguish themselves from others, and begin to hate those persons. Why? You would say it is culture (nurture). I say there is no culture where man is not. Nothing can happen among men that does not reside within men. You wanted me to "pluralize" my thinking and accept both sides. I go one better and ask you to multiplex your thinking and see that man runs from the R complex through the limbic through the neocortex, and that therefore he is capable of almost an infinite variety of expression. It is not an either/or proposition. I accept the totality of mankind's potential.

I never have and never will suggest that male hominids were selected for violence and the territoriality I mentioned. I care nothing for "selection" and all that Darwinist stuff. When I talk about territoriality, I talk about the will to live. I must have food to live. I must compete with other animals (in preagricultural times) and sometimes the other tribes for food. I must compete with other men for the right to breed with the choicest females.

I don't understand why violence or aggressiveness is incompatible with sociability, art, altruism, or whatever. In fact, I look around and see that they coexist. I'm violent and aggressive at times, but I am capable of every other human emotion and deed as well. In fact, I would suggest that you can't enjoy the higher sentiments of the neocortex unless you have the dark underside as well. Can you name one great civilization which wasn't founded on the bloodshed of others? Don't say the Chinese, because they were military as hell, and dynasties supplanted each other by warfare and economic competition. Don't say India because war shaped and reformulated it several times. Egypt was a warrior empire, demanding tribute from others, suffering periodic conquests by others. The Greek city states produced the Trojan War. Homer certainly had a full concept of war and conquest. Alexander catapulted the Greek city states into the Hellenes, and all the discoveries in the arts and sciences, in philosophy, ethics, religion and political thought came about due to the territorial desires of Alexander. Rome stepped to the plate next with continual expansion militarily. The French, Spaniards, Portuguese, and English sought empires abroad and fought each other.

Cooperation has nothing to do with violence. Wolf packs are mod-

els of cooperation and mutual goodwill. But let another pack come
into a pack's territory and see what happens. The same instincts are in
us. I don't even know what the "hunter hypothesis" is. I just know
that everything alive wants to stay alive. That requires certain built-in
instincts. My adrenalin response to danger is hard wired, and a damn
good thing it is, too. My starting and jumping at serpentine and arach-
nid motion is probably a good thing. Why should my not wanting you
to fuck my wife be evil of me, or represent some Darwinian hypothesis? Why is there a genitive case in every language? Wherever there is
a genitive case there is ownership. Where there is ownership it is either mine or ours or yours or theirs. If territory is unimportant, why
does every man on the face of the globe know what "mine" and
"yours" means?

Again, I say there is a thin veneer between the neocortex and the
limbic system and the reticular complex. They are all part of us. We
must accept it. If we ignore it, we will constantly be assailed by motivations we can't understand or deal with because we have denied that
they exist. It has nothing to do with hunters and warriors. It has to do
with surviving, and these things precede by a long time our becoming
human beings at all. They existed before we did.

On controlling speech to control thought: if I don't use gender neutral speech I'm a shameful sexist. I'm probably a misogynist and probably self-hating because you must hate yourself in order to hate others
and so on. I say this is a crock of shit. I was raised in a time where
Man included all genders. It is difficult for me to remember to say
humankind when that is what I mean, and it sounds awkward to say
chairperson instead of chairman. I don't mean any evil by it. I love
women. I respect women. I always will whether I use the term *mankind*
or *humankind*. Sexists will always be sexists, no matter what you constrain them to say. No one likes to be told what to do or to be told that
what they are doing is wrong or harmful when they have no harmful
intentions. When something is disrespectful in and of itself, like referring to women as bitches, or any of the other host of insulting appella-
tions available, I think we have the right to demand that such speech
be prohibited. Same with racial epithets, but trying to force people to
change relatively harmless speech is probably counterproductive.

I don't think there's a chance in hell you can get me a typewriter.
The reason I think the policy won't change is that not long ago some
people from Indiana CURE met Ed Cohn and asked about it. Cohn
said that there was no chance at all of this policy being changed. He
said the personal typewriters were taken because we made weapons

out of the keys. I think the real reason stems from when Congressman Henry Hyde had all the state attorney generals make a top ten list of frivolous prisoner lawsuits. The aim was to get support for the Prison Litigation Reform Act, which severely limits prisoner rights to file federal lawsuits. The problem was that the prison population was dramatically increasing in the late '80s and early '90s. Electronic typewriters with memories allowed you to make multiple copies of any document. You could mass-mail your complaints. So it was electronic typewriters that they banned first. A few months later they banned them all. I think it's meant to control both how much and how effectively we can access the public and the courts.

I'll be 43 on Sunday. Is your daughter about my age? I'll bet she was excited to have such an opportunity. I would love to see India. The Ganges is such a fabled river. I would love to see it from the delta to the source nowadays. I'd also love to see all the great temples including the one where the thousands of rats live a life of luxury and veneration.

Hope we see each other clearer in the future. I never take debate personally, and sometimes it is the best way to find a point of equilibrium with friends.

Bye,
DW

September 9, 2000

Dear Charles,

I had to borrow this typewriter to write judge Sarah Evans Barker a letter. She is the judge in my federal habeas corpus action filed in the U.S. District Court in Indianapolis. My attorney died on August 15. I found out about it when the attorney general filed a motion to have a status conference on my case to determine what they had to do to get a ruling. They think I've stayed alive too long. So I had to write the judge.

If the judge gave me an adverse ruling at this moment, it would be tantamount to an order for summary execution. Because I don't know how, or upon what grounds, to file an appeal to the 7th Circuit Court of Appeals, I told the judge I need counsel appointed.

I also asked for some reasonable time for any new counsel to be-

Indiana Death Row

WALLACE, DONALD RAY, JR. # 16

EXECUTED BY LETHAL INJECTION 03-10-05 12:23 AM EST

DOB: 09-03-1957 DOC#: 7114 White Male

Vigo County Circuit Court
Judge Hugh D. McQuillan

Venued from Vanderburgh County

Prosecutor: Stanley M. Levco, Robert J. Pigman

Defense: William G. Smock

Date of Murder: January 14, 1980

Victim(s): Patrick Gilligan W/M/30; Teresa Gilligan W/F/30; Lisa Gilligan W/F/5; Gregory Gilligan W/M/4 (No relationship to Wallace)

Method of Murder: shooting with handgun

Summary: As attested by the admission of Wallace to friends after the fact, after burglarizing the home of Ralph Hendricks, he "got greedy" and decided to break into the house next door. However, when he did so, he was surprised to find the family inside. Patrick and Teresa Gilligan and their two children, aged 4 and 5, were confronted by Wallace with a gun. All four were tied up and shot in the head. Wallace would say to friends later that he shot Mr. Gilligan because he was "giving him trouble"; he shot Mrs. Gilligan because she was screaming and he "had to shut her up"; and he shot the children because he "could not let the children grow up with the trauma of not having parents." Wallace then took guns, a CB, a scanner, and other property, all of which was later recovered from or traced to Wallace. (Wallace was found incompetent and confined in a mental hospital for almost 2 years prior to trial)

Trial: Venued to Vigo County (01-24-80); Found Incompetent (05-19-80); Found Competent (09-02-80); Found Incompetent (01-16-81); Competency Hearing (06-10-82, 06-11-82, 06-14-82, 06-16-82, 06-18-82); Found Competent (06-28-82); Insanity Defense filed (07-02-82); Insanity Defense Withdrawn (08-12-82); Voir dire (08-31-82, 09-01-82, 09-02-82, 09-03-82, 09-07-82, 09-08-82, 09-09-82); Jury Trial (09-09-82, 09-10-82, 09-11-82, 09-13-82, 09-14-82, 09-15-82, 09-16-82, 09-17-82, 09-18-82, 09-20-82, 09-21-82, 09-22-82); Verdict (09-22-82); DP Trial (09-23-82); Verdict (09-23-82); Court Sentencing (10-21-82).

Conviction: Murder (4 counts)

Sentencing: October 21, 1982 (Death Sentence)

Aggravating Circumstances: b (1) Burglary; b(8) 4 murders

Mitigating Circumstances: extreme emotional disturbance, loveless, insecure childhood

3. Indiana Death Row. Printout of entry on Donald Ray Wallace, Jr., from the Web site listing all Indian death row inmates.

come familiar with the case. It would not do much good to have new counsel appointed if he or she wasn't adequately prepared. So we'll see what happens. I may be here for less time than anticipated.

In other news, I tried to get someone to find whatever it was you found on the internet about my case. Someone found a case summary for me on some prosecutor's web site. You mentioned a *Rashomon* effect when you read about the victims being tied up and shot in the head. In fact, the man broke free. A struggle ensued. I shot him. Then I flipped and shot everyone. The synopsis you read has serious inaccuracies, as follows:

1. It says that I had made admissions to "friends." The friend (singular) who attributed to me every statement made there was Debbie Durham, my girlfriend at the time. At first she knew nothing. Then in each successive statement she knew more. I don't know why she ended up saying that I had gotten greedy and went to a second house to burglarize it, that I killed the woman because she screamed, and that I killed the kids because I didn't want them to grow up as orphans. I think she was trying to find some kind of justification or excuse for what I had done. I will tell you this: I killed those people, but I never said a single one of those statements attributed to me.
2. It says that the people were home when I broke in. In fact, they returned home while I was in the house. This is an important difference in that I had taken great pains to break open a deadbolt lock so I could escape if anyone returned home, but they chose to come through the door that blocked my exit.
3. It says that I shot the children because I didn't want them to grow up orphans. I never gave any reasons. I wasn't able to admit that I did anything at all until 15 years later.

This is not a case of the *Rashomon* effect. My prosecutor was Stanley Levco, who is still the prosecutor in Vandeburgh Co. You can ask him. Or, if Evansville papers are on file in our local library, check the dates between September 15 to the 25th of 1982, when Levco gave his factual closing argument of what happened in that house on January 14, 1980. Read it, and see if I fudged the facts to suit my purpose, or whether I have a shred of credibility in what I told you in my first letter. I was shocked when I read the internet piece because it's wrong on several accounts. Check it out for yourself. I don't want you to think I lied or altered the facts. Look it up in the official sources.

Yours truly,
DW

Undated note from DW

Why DW says football is mock war.
Two teams: Home vs. Visitors
Offense and Defense
   Line of scrimmage: this is the line from which each play begins. Offensive tries to move it farther down field until it scores; defense tries to hold it where it is or repel it back. "Scrimmage" is an alteration of "Skirmish"—a battle (See Webster's). An offense which features passing is said to mount "an aerial attack." One which features runs is said to mount a "ground attack." An offense which features both has "an evenly balanced attack."
   The Quarterback is called the "Field General." Some player positions include "Guards," "Flankers," and "Tackles."
   The offensive players line up in various "formations" like soldiers. A popular kick return formation is the "Phalanx" or "Wedge" formation. If a game is tied after four quarters, an additional quarter is played to "Sudden Death," i.e., the first team that scores in this period wins.
   When I said that "aggression" is in man, I did not and would not say he was "selected for aggression," only that aggression is one of his facets. So is language, art, poetry, and on and on. These things are mostly post-agricultural developments—they occurred after man was selected. Their span hardly represents an eye-blink on the evolutionary scale.

September 12, 2000

Dear DW,
   Our daughter is indeed close to your age. She is in Atlanta now at the Center for Disease Control (CDC), where she and the other volunteers in the polio campaign have a weeklong orientation program before they leave for assignments in different countries.
   Your letters are difficult to respond to. I don't know anything about brain physiology, but I doubt that you do either. When you say you have little interest in genetics and no knowledge of evolutionary theories, you contradict your assertions about "the R complex" (whatever that is), the limbic system and neocortex. When you say that they are "grafted" on each other you are using a metaphor to assert an evolu-

tionary sequence of some kind. "Instincts," whatever they are, are some kind of genetic disposition to act in particular ways that have given a species an adaptive advantage. In this way, natural selection operates to shape the behavior of the species.

What you don't seem to realize is that the co-evolution of human biology and culture has maximized the role of learning in our species, greatly reducing the role of instincts. This has given us an enormous adaptive advantage compared to other large mammals. You confuse your instinctive "adrenalin response," the famous flight or fight response, with what you seem to think is also an instinctive "not wanting (me) to fuck your wife." The first is a very simple undifferentiated instinctive physiological trait, but the situations that provoke the response are learned: in some communities in India brothers share a wife, in our own society some couples have what they call an "open marriage," Eskimos were said to loan their wives to honored guests for the evening, and so on.

I am sorry that you still fail to see the value in women asking scholars and their students to be more sensitive to the ways that gender prejudices are learned and expressed in ordinary language by occasionally referring to God as Her, by avoiding the generic use of Man, and so on. When we do this we become more aware of our assumptions. This "consciousness raising" is basic educational practice. Getting educated is learning to talk and to write in particular ways. The aim is not "mind control," but to have a liberating experience. The prejudice against women in medical, law, and engineering schools has been largely overcome in the last 20 years, but only because of feminist research and criticism. The assumption that the "hard sciences" (physics, chemistry) and math are masculine subjects has had a negative effect on the ability of girls to learn them. Self-conscious efforts to change that assumption have stimulated beneficial changes in American education.

You of all people, DW, should be in sympathy with the feminists. Their cause is aligned with those of people who oppose the death penalty, racism, gay bashing, and the so-called "drug war," along with the enormous expansion of the prison system it has led to.

Now let me respond to our conversation about sports as symbolic warfare. With the cheerleaders yelling "Fight, team, fight," and the disposition of American culture to war metaphors, you have a good argument. Nevertheless, I disagree. When we talked about this during my visit, I was trying to reject your "hard wired" concepts. I recommended *Homo Ludens* by Jan Huizinger, which argues that human nature and culture are grounded in play. Not play as practice to fight and kill, but creative play in ritual, dance, sport, games, music, art, and theater. True, the subjects of novels, dramas, rituals and dances are often conflicts leading to murder, suicide, and war. Thus, in some sense they may rationalize these activities, and may even be practice to engage in them, but in so far as they are aesthetic performances the aim is cathartic, or to entertain.

I don't think a good case can be made for your claim that games are a symbolic substitute for war because we are hard wired for aggression. We know when we are playing and when we are not, and when we play we are not usually practicing for war. We say, "We are just playing," or "We want to have a good time." What we admire in spectator sports is the skill of the player, which resembles the skill we admire in the dancer. Style, beauty, and the joy of play motivate sports, and the observation of sporting events. The contest between teams is a display of skill, discipline, health, and strength.. The hero of sporting events may be compared to a war hero in our highly militaristic culture, but this is only a conventional metaphor. It is not a motive.

A psychologist, Jean Piaget, wrote *The Moral Development of the Child*, in which he studied the ways that children learn to play. Infants respond early to pi-pie as an adult covers and uncovers her face (an observation Freud made much of), but as they begin to play with toys they don't play with each other. After they are good at talking and begin to seek association with each other, they learn and teach each other the rules to play games. According to Piaget this rule-bound behavior is an essential step in the moral development of the child. At a more advanced stage, children realize that rules are social conventions that they can change by negotiating an agreement with other players. I suppose that a particularly creative child may invent a new game by making up the rules for it, but no child I have known has done this.

I have written a lot of this letter on the day after I started it. Your third letter arrived a day after that, and I am shook-up by it. I will wait to answer, but I should say right away that I did not think you had lied about the murders when I read the summary of your case by the prosecutor's office. The point of *Rashomon*, as I recall the film, was that no one was lying. Each version of the murder was the truth as the participant understood it. I reasoned that you wrote a brief and true description of your life to explain why you were on death row. To include the act of tying up your victims in the climax you would have had to expand the description. Anyone who writes knows that you can't say everything and remain coherent. Also, I knew that the prosecutor wanted to justify the death penalty, and, of course, in my view nothing justifies it.

Sincerely,
Charles

September 19, 2000

Dear Charles,
Hi. I received your latest yesterday, for which thanks. You said it was difficult to respond to my letters. This is probably because I had to type them with such haste. It was almost like writing in the "stream of consciousness" manner, which isn't suitable for scholarly debate. I'll try to do better.

I was disingenuous when I said I knew nothing about Darwinism and cared nothing about genetics. I have a fair overview of both. That's why I avoid them. I have seen the finest minds sink into the cesspool of vain and flatulent theorizing about what woman was selected for. I sought instead to offer measurable and comparable proof, of a physical nature rather than to promote, defend, or debate ideologies.

Darwin claimed that all forms of life descended from a common ancestor, and that the diversity of life in the world today can be accounted for by natural selection. Members of any given species will differ from each other, and from this variety nature will then select those best adapted to their environment to survive and bear offspring. Most scientists believe Darwin's treatise was generally accurate. They've added what woman now knows about genetics in a synthesis called neo-Darwinism. But huge internal disputes fairly roll about the respective roles in evolution of chance, adaptation, selection, genes, individual organisms, groups, struggle, competition, cooperation, et cetera ad nauseam. These are the very disputes I'd rather not muddy my shoes in.

I have no more than 50 or 60 hours of study of brain physiology, which isn't a lot. But I wanted to make the simple point that woman is just another animal and shares certain traits and characteristics with her animal kindred, mammalian and even reptilian. If I threw two amygdalae, one from a horse and one from woman, on a table you would not find anything to distinguish them from each other. They act and relate to each respective brain in the same way, and produce the same general output upon the same stimulus. The horse also has a neocortex, but it's fortunately not big enough to make horses think they are some kind of transcendent beings whose penchant for dreaming up myriads of opposing ideologies makes them different from all their animal kin.

True, a horse's smaller neocortex makes the amygdale's output more dominant in a horse's behavior. Woman can suppress or sublimate her amygdala's output and turn it into an achievement, individual or cooperative. My point is that deep inside we react like a horse to the same things a horse reacts to. Our cortices diffuse and rechannel that emotional and motivational energy into all the human channels.

I say, with respect to all this, that football and boxing and gladiators somehow address these animal impulses. As man evolves they become less real and more ritualized.

My point with using physical systems is the undeniable comparative effect of showing that the adrenal cortex crowning a horse's kidney is identical in form and function to the one crowning my kidney. They produce the same chemical for the same purpose. You say my fight or flight concept is confused with ideas such as not wanting you to fuck my wife, or move uninvited into my living room, or eat all my food. Let's look at one of your examples, the Eskimos.

Oh, but first, your comment that you "doubt that I know anything about brain physiology either" was funny. I bet Darwin was amused when you wrote that to him when he was a young man. You have a sharp tongue in debate, don't you? Do keep on, though, I'll add these to my learned behaviors of what to say when my hierarchical dominance trigger is flipped.

Anyway—Eskimos lived in small and isolated compounds, and long winters often prevented intertribal movement. Consequently, the problem of recessive traits and other genetic problems associated with a small gene pool would quickly become apparent. So it could easily be reasoned that the instinct for self preservation outweighed the usual sexual competition urge. As I've read about this practice I believe that the definition of an "honored guest" was that he was male, strong, clear-eyed, and intelligent. But we are knee deep in the neo-Darwinian dunghill I wanted to avoid. My opinion hasn't been altered by anything you've presented, and I'm sure I haven't caused you to repent your opinion. That's why logic is every man's favorite girlfriend. She'll let you do whatever you want as often as you like.

You will note that I've tried to use the feminine pronoun in this letter to show that I love and respect women and that I get the point. But I will not continue to do this if I am told I should or must do it for whatever reason. I reserve the right to think my own thoughts and to order them in speech as I will to do. I am teachable. I listen to reasonable debate, but I have to remain free to choose to agree, disagree, or straddle the fence. If you try to force me to do anything I will rebel. This is my nature, confirmed by my consistent actions over many years. I do not respond well to force.

Emotional blackmail is a type of force. To say I should do whatever feminists require me to do because they support causes dear to me is unpersuasive. Sorry, but my flight/fight trigger is forever stuck on fight. I hate force being applied against me in any form. Thanks for looking into the status of my case. Judge Evans-Barker is supposed to be a very fair judge. I doubt she'll accede to the state's demand for a ruling without me being adequately represented by counsel. But I don't know. In a way, I don't mind dying. Twenty years in prison has been a hell beyond recounting.

Until next time,
DW

September 22, 2000

Dear Charles,

You mentioned that in your youth you wanted to be an artist. Did you ever follow up on that—art as a hobby? I'm enclosing a piece I did. The style is heavy and distorted. Usually I'm finer and more photo-realistic in style. But I like to try different things.

What I do best is play guitar. I wish you could hear me. I impress even myself, and I'm a very critical person. Thanks to you I'm playing lately with a shiny new set of strings. Nothing is sweeter than a new set of strings!

Do you follow the Olympic Games? It's strange that this year's summer games are in Australia, where the first day of spring occurred yesterday. Everything is backwards in Australia. The Europeans who settled it were convicts instead of Puritans. So they don't have the good sensibilities down there to spend millions of dollars and thousands of hours of government time trying to impeach officials for having healthy libidos. I think during the Clinton-Lewinski fiasco an

4. Art deco-style drawing.

Australian official said, "Thank God our country was settled by Felons!"

I got an order from Judge Barker today. She has instructed an Indianapolis attorney named Sarah L. Nagy to review my file to see if she wants to take my case. I've never heard of her, but she's probably good for that reason. We know all of the state-owned public defenders. So this is good news.

If we argue nature vs. nurture until our lower mandibles fall off, I hope we can nevertheless be friends. I hope you can see that I'll argue only with people I like. I don't talk at all to people I don't like. I also don't joke with people I don't like, so the crack about you being old enough to have said the same thing to Darwin as you said to me is a sign of affection.

Yours truly,
DW

Saturday, September 30, 2000

Dear DW,

On Monday I returned from Berkeley, where I attended a fascinating 3-day conference called "Who owns the body?" I had purchased a book on the Qabalah for you after reading a favorable review in the *N.Y. Times*, and read it during the trip. I mailed it this week: *Dreams of Being Eaten Alive: The Literary Core of the Kabbalah*, translated by David Rosenberg. Once years ago I paused in library stacks to read some medieval Jewish literature. It gave detailed instructions on how to get undressed at night, which side of the bed to get into, which side your wife should be on, how to enter her and not to talk during intercourse, how to urinate and defecate properly, exactly how to take a bath, and so on. Nothing was left in ordinary life to be done spontaneously. In short, a great prison of ritual, every move locked in. This book wasn't that way, but is composed of snippets from the Qabalah to illustrate its aesthetic properties.

When I got back I had a letter from a lawyer I talked to at the ACLU dinner, Chris Hitz-Bradley, Deputy Public Defender, at the office of Public Defender of Indiana. He checked the rule about not replacing your typewriter, and said that I could write to Superintendent Rondle L. Anderson.

I am not pissed by your strictures. I was surprised that you took offense when I wrote that I don't know anything about brain anatomy/physiology, and didn't think you did either. I am accustomed to acknowledging the fact that such subjects require long training with extensive laboratory research, and that the scientists who are trained in them disagree with each other on many critical issues. I was debating with you to bring you down to my level, where, on the whole, anthropologists are suspicious of claims about instinctual behavior.

Sorry to be so brief.

Good wishes,
Charles

October 5, 2000

Dear Charles,

Hi. Thanks for your latest. Sarah Nagy took my case. She seems very competent. A lawyer once said this to me: "You ask your client if she did it, and you hope she's smart enough to say no." I've followed his advice. So you are privy to information that Ms. Nagy won't have, and I hope you'll keep it that way. She seems honest and nice, but so does everyone when you first meet them, lawyers most of all. I may tell her the whole truth in time. I don't know.

I'm sure I'll enjoy the Qabala book. I practice a very syncretic form which takes the intellectual models of the Qabala—the Tree of Life, for example—as mnemonic systems. There are 32 paths on the Tree: 10 spheres and 22 paths connecting them. Each sphere represents an idea, a heading under which you can file and compare all like phenomena. I'll explain this better in another letter.

You can forget the typewriter letter. There are three loaner typewriters in my section. Prisoners keep them. We can borrow them, but if you write Anderson he'll just say that there are loaner typewriters. He cannot suspend a rule that his boss, Ed Cohn, enacted. Moreover, if the police come and take the loaner typewriters from the prisoners who keep them it will be even harder to borrow them. Believe me, I know from experience. So, thanks, but I'll make out without a typewriter of my own.

More later,
DW

Oct 9, 2000

Dear DW,

Thank you for the version you made of a famous art deco design. This is one of my favorite styles. The music school at Indiana University has a handsome art deco building, which at one time was the Bloomington high school. Rockefeller Center is a splendid example of the style. When I was growing up, art deco penthouses and nightclubs were the setting in which Fred Astaire and Ginger Rogers danced. Architecture, furniture, sculpture, paintings, jewelry and household objects were made in this style during the 1920s and '30s. I think the design that inspired your drawing was etched on a glass panel.

We will be leaving for southern Italy on October 31 and returning on December 3. We are going on a tour devoted to Greek and Roman antiquity, with visits to archaeological sites and museums. My wife's family is from the Veneto region in the north. On previous visits to Italy we have not gotten south of Rome, so this trip will be a special treat.

We get e-mails from our daughter in India. Although she spent her junior and senior high school years in northern India and learned to speak Hindi, she is stationed in southern India, where Kanada is spoken. The town she uses as a home base has a cyber café. Thus, we have instant communication. This is an astonishing contrast to the period of my fieldwork. I used a small portable typewriter, it took ten days or more for letters to the U.S., and we expected to wait a month for a reply.

I would like to find a way to be helpful to you. Could I contact your sisters, who you said have shown concern for you, or other family members or friends interested in your welfare? Since we will be leaving soon there is little time for me to do a this, but I am certainly willing to do what I can, and perhaps get a start on something that can be followed up when we return.

Yours truly,
Charles

3

Qabalah

Dear Charles,

Thanks for the efforts you made in my behalf, but don't trust the state Public Defender. I know you will think this is an ignorant or biased opinion. They are more of your social class, share college educations with you, and so forth. They belong in good liberal organizations with you. They are probably very nice. They no doubt donate money to good causes. So you will naturally think anything I say against them is wrong—especially in light of the fact that I maintain that human beings display instinctive behavior which seems to cross cultural boundaries. You probably therefore already think I'm ignorant, and if I say something against your class compatriots you'll probably just add it to the list of reasons why I'm confused.

Here's the deal. The Public Defender receives her payroll from the Indiana Supreme Court. Susan Carpenter frequently dines with Chief Justice Randal Shepard, ostensibly to talk about budgetary matters. This is a fact: several times he has told her not to file certain arguments in cases coming before the court. She comes back and tells her chief deputies not to file those issues. They pass it on. They will not go after incompetent or ineffective attorneys. They will not go after prosecutors who engaged in gross misconduct. They will not rock the boat. The flip side of this is that the other side never stops doing those things. They do whatever is necessary to convict you and keep you convicted. The Public Defenders do whatever is necessary to keep from causing trouble. They are pathetic. I don't want anything to do with Susan Carpenter or her office.

As far as Qabalah goes, you are not likely to find anything instructive in the popular media. The good stuff is taught to the "listening ear" from the "instructive mouth." Some things are never to be written down, and what is written down often makes no sense without direct oral instruction. I've been sworn to secrecy on such matters. The secrets do not have momentous value, but it is a matter of fraternity, personal honor, and the power of secrecy, which is important.

There are pure Jewish Qabalists, like the Hasidim. There are some twenty other schools, and none of them agree on so much as whether it should be spelled in English Qabalah, Kabalah, or Cabalah. The h on the end of the word can be omitted at times—as a suffix it indicated the quality of holiness. For example Abram became Abraham, and Sara became Sarah. It is always a mystical system, and sometimes a magical system. In some parts it purports to comprehend a secret subtext in the Torah. In other parts it uses a system of numerology for interpretations and magical ceremonies.

Religious exercises can be a sort of magic. The magic I believe in is the power to change yourself. When you do this, the universe is changed correspondingly. Actually, the universe is the same, but your change enables you to see it in a different way.

There is so much to Qabalah that I can't begin to recount its themes here. The part I concern myself with has been set forth into the Western Occult Tradition: The Tree of Life (Eitz ha-Chaim) and its symbolism. It is represented by the enclosed diagram. The Jewish Qabalists proposed that its ten spheres embody the progressive emanations of God from the three veils of negative existence to the sense matter of our world (the accursed world of shells). I look at it rather as the constitution, or body, of man

The Tree of Life expresses ideas that escape regular phraseology. It is an instrument for interpreting symbols whose meaning has become obscure. This is accomplished by connecting forms, sounds, and numbers to corresponding spiritual, moral, or intellectual values. The system of correspondences tests the truth of new ideas in the light of their coherence with the whole body of knowledge. Practice leads to refinement, through experience rather than book learning. The spheres and paths have Tarot symbols, which in turn have astrological and planetary symbols, which have nothing to do with actual stars or planets in the heavens.

This may seem confusing to you and not productive of benefit. I make no claims about it except that I practice it. I will explain it to you if you wish, but I won't debate it. Books about it are nearly useless. Gersham Scholem has written the best ones. New Agers have a problem of credulity since they take the symbols literally.

On the brain physiology thing our problem might be our different backgrounds. I've seen time and again how quickly social pleasantries

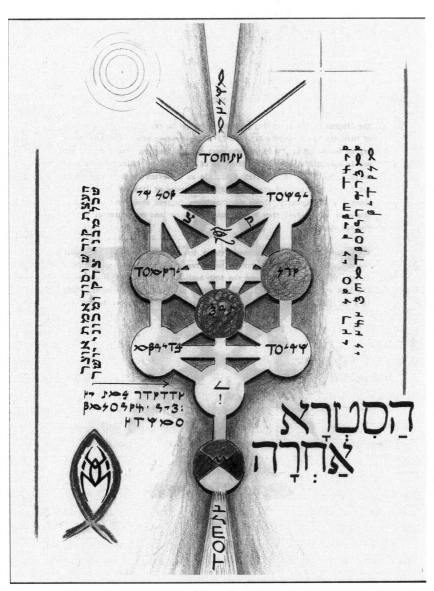

5. Tree of life.

and conventions dissipate when stress comes. Then idealizing dissipates like smoke, and the truth is revealed. If I set up a tent in your front yard and acted like I owned that spot, I don't think your irritation would be cultural. I wasn't truly pissed by your remark that I probably didn't know much about brain physiology. I did interpret it as a shot, though, so I responded in kind. That's how I debate. If the debate turns to insults, I don't take the high road but give it right back. If someone thinks they are of a class of people who morally should not be hit, then they should not hit me. I'm an equal opportunity retaliator.

Your friend,
DW

October 20, 2000

Dear Charles,

I received your card and the $50 today, for which many thanks. I like the card's Northwest Coast Indian art. You treat me better than I deserve. I act like an asshole a lot of the time.

As for honesty being the best policy, I agree, but if I never tell Sarah Nagy I am guilty then she is ethically and legally free to put on any reasonable evidence of my innocence. If I tell her I did it, then she could be disbarred for knowingly putting on false evidence or suborning perjury from possible witnesses. That's why attorneys always ask, but hope you're smart enough to say you didn't do it.

To tell you the truth, I don't want any part of the 240-year sentence I would receive in lieu of a death sentence. I've been locked up for 20 years, that's enough. I'm not afraid to die. I may be afraid to keep living like this.

I didn't know the genesis of my drawing. I saw it on a little 2" × 3" photocopy on a catalog. It wasn't very well reproduced, but I was struck by it enough that I knew I wanted to draw it. I love art deco. It looks "futuristic" even today. There's a simple elegance to it, and I like the way it uses both curves and angles to work its magic.

Do you like Frank Lloyd Wright architecture? He's my favorite. He did some art deco stuff. His house called Falling Water was built right over a stream in the woods. It has a faintly art deco look.

I admire the sense of awe and mystery with which the ancients viewed the world. Even if it is ignorant to believe in gods and spirits, a world peopled with them is fraught with meaning. Now it is difficult to find meaning in existence. We are the products of random chance, with no purpose greater than ourselves. Life is sadder now.

Have a good trip to Europe,
DW

October 26, 2000

Dear DW,
The kind of things that you find spiritually useful are not in the Qabala book I mailed to you.

I enclose a clipping on baseball from the *New York Times* this morning. It caused me to think of the identification of sports with democracy. Games are egalitarian. The players are equally subject to the rules (they have "an even playing field"), and the contest is ruined if they are not "equally matched." The winner has "achieved status," which democratic societies value, in contrast to the "ascribed status" of nationality, gender, and family heritage. The symbolism of military conquest emphasizes the victor's domination of the defeated enemy, while the "good sport" winners and losers respect each other. Instead of valuing equal contests, military combat initiates unequal contests and tries to "take advantage" of the rules rather than honoring them. Thus, the military use of surprise attacks like Pearl Harbor, the arms race for military superiority (which the U.S. brags about all the time), the use of spies and satellite spy technology, the concept of military secrets and so on. While war is often used as a metaphor for sport contests, they have a different character.

I wonder why you do not mention getting the Qabala book. It emphasizes the poetic qualities of Qabala texts. It also has a bibliography and discussion of issues of interpretation. The author/translator is a prominent Jewish scholar.

Your friend,
Charles

November 12, 2000

Dear Charles,

Greetings. I hope your trip abroad was enjoyable. Aside from all the obvious regrets in my life, I regret that I couldn't travel around the world to see Rio during Carnival, or Cairo at night from the top of the Great Pyramid, or to walk along the shores of the Dead Sea, see the Qumran caves and the buildings carved from stone cliffs at Petra. To see the old Chinese temples and towns along the Yangtze River before they flood it all with the new dam. So many wonderful places and fascinating people. How in God's name did I get locked into the path my life took?

The election of the president isn't settled yet. The Florida count will decide who won. As I see it, neither candidate offers any fundamental change.

I received *Dreams of Being Eaten Alive* right after I wrote you last. Thanks. It's a nice book. The poetic and allegorical aspect of Qabalah is important, but I can tell you this: Qabalah can never be grasped by reading books. It is a journey or quest.

The *New York Times* op/ed piece on the rules of baseball was interesting, as were your remarks on games. I agree. Rules are important in sporting contests, but what do humans admire in warriors? Daring. Cunning. Bravery. Intelligence. Deceit is fundamental in war. You try to fool your enemy. Same with football. The play action pass is when you fake like you mean to run the ball and when the defense responds to the run you pass instead. In baseball, pitchers throw breaking balls, curves, sliders, forkballs, and change-ups. The object is to deceive. There is all kind of deception in every sporting contest, and an athlete's ability to sell a feint is admired all around. My point is that I can agree with you and the op/ed writer and still be firmly convinced that sporting contests are analogs of war.

I've been thinking about our discussion a lot. The question may be more one of what instinct is exactly than anything else. Is the aggression that creates wars in every civilization instinctive? And if it is instinctive, is it also the cause for sporting contests?

It is easy to identify what is instinctive in, say, a caterpillar spinning a cocoon. It was not taught to do it, yet caterpillars invariably perform this elaborate act. I read somewhere that biologists conducted experiments on caterpillars in the process of cocoon building by interrupting their labor and placing them on other cocoons both less and more constructed than the cocoon on which they'd been working. Fascinating results were noted, and it is easy to identify this as instinctive.

Now, what if caterpillars developed the capacity for abstract thought and philosophy? They would still build cocoons, but they would invent all kinds of reasons for the activity. Some caterpillars would declare that cocoons were ordained by God Almighty, and there'd be some creation myth or story about the Great Cocoon. Others would say the universe was material and governed by chance and that cocoon building was selected by the vagaries of existence. Others would claim it came from archetypal dreams of the womb and the bliss therein of the mythical garden of Eden. There'd be great tomes of theories about it.

Let's take it a step farther. What if they learned to build permanent dwellings in the shape of cocoons that were passed down from generation to generation? There would be no need to build a cocoon, but the urge, nameless and haunting, would still be within them. They might develop strange arts and crafts to try to satisfy this inborn urge. If it went on for a long time, these arts and crafts might become so unlike cocoons that you couldn't recognize them as such. Periodically, cocoon building might break out in times of natural disaster, or among deviants or anarchists. No one would connect this actual cocoon building with the bizarre arts and crafts. One day caterpillar Donald would say, "You know, I think these strange boxes the artist caterpillars create are nothing more or less than sublimated cocoon building." Caterpillar Charles would say, "No, no! The boxes represent what is good in caterpillarism, and what is noble in the race. Caterpillars don't have instincts, only animals do!"

How do you recognize an instinct when it becomes buried in the nonsense of thought?

It is just as logical to favor the death penalty as it is not to favor it. We have been arguing about it without any end. The respective biases of each side prevent them from seeing the other side as anything but just plain wrong. Some of us are so compartmentalized that we can kill one person in one circumstance but cry out against killing someone else in a circumstance very similar. We can kill the Nuremburg Nazis because they were inherently evil, but in America we shouldn't kill a mass murderer because he's just a misunderstood product of his culture. We should be better than that.

At every new stage, people will debate the same things anew. Most people see the parts of things but not the whole. I look at sports and see war and warriors. You look at sports and see civilizations. The difference is that I never said that sport is nothing but war. I said that it was sublimated war. When I say something is sublimated I mean that it has been placed under other conditions.

We can have champions face each other in single combat to determine the winning of certain spoils. In fact, we need not have our warriors fight to the death. Once a year we might gather under flags of truce and hold contests to determine glory (bragging rights) and booty. Our spirit of competition might make one boast that "our warriors are superior spearmen." We'd make a spear contest, something like the javelin throw.

Another might boast, "Our warriors are the fastest runners." If defeated in a short sprint, he might amend, "Over the long distance, our runners are superior." Pretty soon you'd have all sorts of foot races.

"Our warriors are stronger!" Wrestling.

"Our warriors jump higher." High jump.

Soon warriors are not warriors but athletes who train for some specialized war-derived contest. I know that Freud said that sometimes a cigar is just a cigar, but if a javelin is not a spear, what is it? "Athlete" comes from a Greek word signifying "one who contends for a prize," from the verb signifying "to contend." At the time when the word came into use, no one capable of being an athlete could refuse to be also a warrior. Only cowards did not fight as warriors. Guess what the main training devices of the Spartans were? That's right, athletic contests among the warriors. These were used both to train for actual war and also to sift out the strongest, quickest, and most cunning for leadership positions. Read the histories. Most of the games of the Olympics (before they added beach volleyball and all that) were invented by Greek soldiers.

The advantages of sublimating the instinct to make war are countless. We can get off our aggression without penalty. We make and enforce stern rules so that things don't get out of hand and spark actual battles. Now we can trade with our enemy while still reviling him, or feeling superior to him, or being aggrieved that his warriors somehow cheated in the last contest. But next year, well, look out! The communities flourish: stability allows long-term planning, libraries and universities to come into existence, and the fruit of one's labor can be passed on to the offspring or back to the community. We can release all our hostilities and aggressions in the big sporting tournaments at year's end. We might come to like this arrangement so much that we grow closer to our enemies and forget for a time that they are enemies. We might even forget what started the contests or why we looked forward to them so much every year. (But caterpillar Donald would know!)

The war between the North and South has been over for more than 125 years, but the memory of enmity is not forgotten. There is to this very day an annual Blue vs. Gray football game where all stars from colleges are picked to represent their respective war colors. (Caterpillar Donald observes and takes note not of what might possibly be in the best of all worlds, but what is in the world in which he in fact dwells.) The vanquished remember the longest. The South has not forgotten the War between the States. The battles are sublimated, to the advantage of all. Yet war and aggression are the subtext. (Caterpillar Donald distills all these things down to a simple formulae for those parched in throat for understanding. Drink! Imbibe! Caterpillar Donald begrudges no fellow worm a drink of the wine of wisdom! If any are lucky, they'll quickly grow right drunk from it as he himself is drunk on the ale of being so right all the time! O woe is he, to be right in a world so wrong!)

Till next time. Peace
DW

December 1, 2000

Dear Charles,

I've enjoyed the cards from Italy. Nothing new here. My Greek gets better every day. I've also begun to learn Egyptian hieroglyphic language. It seems pretty easy. I think I have a gift for languages.

Yours truly,
DW

New Year's Day, 2001

Dear Charles,

Greetings, friend. It is always a happy thing to be able to greet friends at the turn of a new year. I never know if this is my last year or not—none of us truly do—and I would guess at your age you share a similar familiarity with the idea of one's mortality. So let us live and celebrate life, that precious thing we often take for granted.

I know that it is technically your turn to write. But I had the strangest and most vivid dream a couple of nights ago. You and I were on a lake in a boat, fishing. As usual, we were debating the natures of men and beasts. As usual without much success in persuading each other, either. But it was with a pleasant tone, and we enjoyed the fishing. Suddenly, you hooked a big fish and began to reel it in. When it got close to the boat, I dipped a net into the water to retrieve your catch. It was a gigantic large-mouth bass. I unhooked it, and it spoke, saying, "I heard you two debating the nature of man." I dropped the fish in astonishment. It simply looked up at us and continued to talk.

"The problem," said the fish, "is that you are each only looking at one side. Man has two main motivating themes. One is the hope of gain. That is the side you see, Donald. The hope of gain manifests in many ways, such as wealth, power, fame, freedom, or security. But the other motivation in Man is the need to make sense out of the universe. That is the side Charles sees. Not only is this side the source of every religion and myth ever formulated, but it also inspires every philosophy and morality. Two are the moons of man's madness, and it seems as though one always wanes when the other waxes, so that neither beholds the other. Man, I name thee Box and Cox: and now ask who is the shrewd landlady who deceives you? Now I've done you a good turn, and nor beast nor god fails to recognize kindness. Throw me back into the lake, and think on what I've said."

So we threw the fish back into the lake, and didn't talk for a long time. Then I awakened and tried to write it all down as best I could. What I've written is not exactly what the fish said. It may have said more or less, and it may have used different words. But I think I got the gist of it.

In any case, it was the most lucid dream I've had in years, so I thought I would share it with you. I haven't too much tried to analyze it—it may have been no more than a piece of moldy bread for supper!

Happy New Year to you and Zelda and all your family!

Yours truly
DW

2
The Year 2001

4

Myths and Reason

January 1, 2001

Dear DW,

We are back from Italy on December 3. I finished a short entry for the *Encyclopedia Britannica*, as usual battling writer's block by rewriting every sentence numerous times. I hope you got my Christmas card with a postal money order.

Now that the holidays are over I will settle down with your long letter. I suppose we have exhausted the clarification of our differences on nature and nurture as sources of human aggression. So what else can we argue about?

Tom Miller answered an e-mail to say he might come here. I offered to meet him at the airport, and put him up. Then we could drive to Michigan City to visit you and Kevin. Before that, I will make the trip alone to visit you.

You do not respond to my request to tell me how to contact your family. Are they still in Indiana? Would one of your sisters or some other relative or friend want to come with me to visit you? It is a four-hour drive each way, so I would like to have company on the trip. Also, of course, I would like to join with someone else who is concerned for your welfare. I am curious to meet your friends or family members, just to talk about you with them.

Did I tell you that I have been going to the Bloomington prison on Tuesday evenings to visit prisoners? The prison minister sets the time, and the other people who go carry Bibles. The prisoners come to a large room, some of them also clutching Bibles. I don't study the Bible myself, and only want to meet them to show concern for their problems. Frequently they proselytize me. They are very poor. Anyone with a little money would be out on bail. Their crimes for the most part are drunken driving, petty theft, dealing drugs, and parole violations. They mention having been arrested a number of times. They

71

might break out of that pattern if we made less use of prisons and put more effort in helping troubled people establish constructive lives.

Of course, if your greatest hope is to get high and party, and if you don't have money and don't want to work, no matter what do-gooders think, you are going to get into trouble with the law.

Things were different in the Zapotec community we studied years ago. On the whole, townspeople considered Mexican officials to be corrupt and hostile. Any dealing with them required bribes, and they often treated Indians with contempt. Within the community, occasional violent fights and several murders occurred during the year we lived there. Everyone knew everything about these events, but if outside authorities turned up nobody would admit to knowing anything. The man who killed another left town almost at once, going to live in a mountain village until things cooled off. Much depended on who the murdered man was and the circumstances of the act. If the murdered man was not respected—if he had a violent reputation, was said to steal things, had failed to perform community work that everyone was responsible for, people did not much blame the killer, and he could soon return home. If the killer and his victim were drunk, many townspeople would consider the death an accident. The prison had only two rooms, and they were used to isolate people while they sobered up or cooled off. This system of maintaining order meant that any man who lost respect as a member of the community, and whose behavior was threatening, was liable to be killed by anyone he offended. The Mexican government's police, courts, and prisons were avoided as alien and corrupt institutions, and townspeople prided themselves for their peacefulness, solidarity, and good manners. Even so, of course, conflicts and ill feelings were a constant source of gossip. Did I send you a copy of my book on the town?

Thanks for your Christmas card. It doesn't seem logical to wish you a happy New Year, but who knows? Maybe something good will happen to you in 2001.

Sincerely,
Charles

January 18, 2001

Dear Charles,

Hi. I'm finally recovering from a terrible cold which hit me on the 4th of this month. It really hung around for a long time.

As for "the argument," I thought we had merely gotten past clarifying our positions and were only beginning a debate that might last for years. I kind of hate to start new arguments until the old ones run their course.

As for contacting my family, basically I only get along with one sister. She can't drive on the highway because a childhood head injury left her with grand mal seizures triggered by rhythmic visual stimuli, like strobe lights or highway center lines. Moreover, I'm very compartmentalized in dealing with people. Every relationship is separate to me and comes with its own terms, boundaries, and finds its own equilibrium. When you start mixing them together you get into more complex social dynamics that baffle and distress me.

So, you have visited prisoners in the Bloomington jail. Unlike you, I'm versed in the Christian Bible, including the original Greek, which gives a better feel for some things. My take on it is that much of it is a collation of myths and sayings attributed to Jesus, who may not have existed. It is a synthesis of desert/Semitic religions of "Law" with Hellenic concepts of philosophy. At least, that's my take on the four synoptic gospels. As for the Pauline doctrines and the other epistles, I think they apply to the priesthood of a sect in the tradition of all sects of that day, and not to ordinary folk such as you and I.

You ask if criminals might do better if we used prisons less, etc. My question is, why is crime in this country so much more than in others? Is there something fundamentally wrong with our nation? I think that every empire has a lifespan. It may be that a social evolution proceeds just as surely as a physical one does and that war, poverty, oppression, racism, class prejudice, etc., must continue until they simply die out. Right now these things seem thoroughly ingrained in the nature of man.

You will immediately recognize that this falls right at the heart of our nature vs. nurture debate. If you think that humanity's evils are only cultural aberrations that can be corrected, then you can't agree that we have to endure them. If you believe like I do, that culture proceeds from man's nature, then you will agree that we have to wait for man's nature to change. I would rather that you were right—that we could simply preach the good word to people and they'd see the error of their ways and we'd all live happily ever after. I can't believe that will happen.

The Zapotec system of justice seems superior to me. Tribal people evolve in wisdom whereas Westerners evolve in their ability to manipulate things but lack wisdom. Tribal people think of the whole. We think of the individual. A few years ago some Northwestern Indians disciplined two teenagers by setting them on different islands for a year to live alone. They would be periodically checked on, and some supplies were sent. The idea was that they realize how good it was to be a part of the tribe, and to adjust their behavior accordingly. Even when you realize how much you'd like to be back in good stead, our society won't let you back in. "Have you ever been convicted of a felony?" is an omnipresent question on a job application. The Indian boys are back home, members of the tribe. American ex-cons can hardly ever come back home.

Americans are hypnotized by self-righteousness. They start with the premise that they are always right. They say, "We may not have a perfect justice system, but it's the best system in the world!" People repeat that who have never seriously studied even an other justice system. When you've had smoke blown up your ass all your life about how superior your society is compared to all others, how can you have a clear picture of things?

I hope all is well with you and yours,
DW

January 31, 2001

Dear DW,

Your use of the talking fish story from the book of selections from the Qabala that I sent you was amusing.

Could my wife, Zelda, get a permit to visit you with me? If so, send me a form for her to fill out. She has been reading your letters and would like to visit you if we could do it together.

I have been working on a paper for a medical anthropology journal. The first version was sent for peer review to three anonymous scholars. They thought it should be lengthened. When I write for publication I feel inadequate—as if I were a fraud and the readers will find me out. To make it longer I have to read several books that I should have read already, and reread others. I must write something that will interest people who know more than I do. It is painful, until I get into it, then I start feeling better.

Now, money. It is always useful. I respect your not asking me for any. I will get to the post office for a money order.

Charles

February 15, 2001

Dear DW,

I hoped that by now we would have a form so that my wife can visit you with me. You wrote that you do not want to deal with more than one person at a time when I asked about your sister. Does that apply as well to Zelda?

If you still want to debate the nature/nurture thing, just write something else I will consider wrong-headed or misinformed and I will respond. I thought we had finished that topic because your letters indicated that you understood my position, and I understand yours. You said that you will not be persuaded, and neither will I.

Sincerely,
Charles

February 28, 2001

Dear DW,

Monday was not a good day. I drove 434 miles to Michigan City and back for a brief visit with you. I waited 45 minutes once I got to the prison, then the guards took time making me remove my leg brace before they would let me in. Actually, they were patting down all the prison employees as they entered and left, so I didn't feel discriminated against, though on previous visits they had not made me remove the brace.

I wrote the governor urging a moratorium before the execution of your friend Gerald Bivins and mailed a copy to Bivins. An article in the paper yesterday reported that he and another prisoner attacked a guard. Tom sent me an e-mail saying that Kevin was also involved, and put in solitary.

I haven't gotten the letter you said was in the mail. Maybe it will come before we leave town. It will be interesting to see the list you order things from. I would not have thought to send you money in the first place if my son had not needed spending money while he was in a federal prison for growing marijuana. It was a minimum security prison, and he wore out shoes playing tennis! It was the sort of prison where they send people who embezzle millions, or senators who take bribes. When we drove to Pennsylvania to see him, the parking lot at his prison would be full of Lincoln Continentals, Cadillacs, and Mercedes. The cars were very different from the aging and banged up wrecks that dominate the parking lot at your prison.

Father and son embezzlers from Brooklyn were given kosher food that was better than the regular fare. The father, in his late 70s, said that prison was as good as retiring in Florida, with the additional advantage of being free! My son thought that he should have asked for kosher food when he was admitted, claiming to be an Italian Jew. Even so, it was a bad experience.

I was surprised to see you with your hair loose rather than in a ponytail. It made your face look thinner. Or, have you lost weight?

Your friend,
Charles

February 28, 2001

Dear Charles,

Thanks for the money order. I haven't felt much like writing. My friend Gerald Bivins waived his appeals and is scheduled to die on March 14. I've been depressed.

I'm enclosing a visitor approval form for Zelda. It will take a couple of weeks after she sends it to be approved. They will send me the approval notice and I'll mail it that day. I would like to meet her.

Well, yes, we've clearly outlined our positions on nature vs. nurture. But that doesn't mean we can't learn anything new by arguing.

I hope you have a great time in London. I look forward to more postcards.

Your friend,
DW

April 7, 2001

Dear DW,

I am glad we stopped to visit you on our way to Chicago for the funeral of Zelda's cousin. He was 87 and had been ill for some time. The funeral was very Italian, with an open casket that people, including children, went up to for a close view and to touch the corpse, if they were so inclined. The banquet after the funeral was festive, with stories about outrageous things the dead man had done, e.g., he once lost his restaurant in a poker game, along with his wife's horse and a fine saddle.

It is good that you and Zelda met. When we left the prison I asked her what her impression was of you. She said that you were gentle. This surprised me, but I understood. During our visit, when I said, "You are wrong," aggressively I admit, I saw the startled look in your face. That look, like a mirror, showed me my own abrasive manner.

I sent you a subscription to *The New York Review of Books*. It will come every two weeks, except in the summer. Besides reviews that discuss books in detail by putting them in the context of other works, the *Review* has articles on political issues, or about prominent authors and artists. You may not like it very much but still find a few essays that interest you.

Yours,
Charles

April 7, 2001

Dear Charles,

Greetings. We're in the second week of the "cell standardization" lockdown. I enjoyed meeting Zelda. I can see why you were so taken with her.

In our continuing debate, I think we really got to the crux of the issue when you said that you wanted to "demythologize" society to form a civilization built on reason. Socrates, according to Plato in *The Republic*, wanted pretty much the same thing. I come from a different perspective. I wish there were more myth and wonder in life. Reason alone seems sterile to me. Ultimately science is a sort of faith that pro-

claims the universe and everything has no purpose, and therefore neither do we.

To argue against your position I would like to clarify it first. For
example, what reason is there for men to climb Mr. Everest? It is dangerous and serves no purpose at all. Yet look how many tried. Recently
they found poor Mallory's bones. What did he die for? The world re-
joiced when Hillary and Tensing Norgay finally conquered the mountain. What did they achieve? Not a damn thing, really. They got to
the top of a land formation before anyone else. And, true to form, it
created political turmoil. The Nepalese wanted Norgay to say that it
was in fact he, and not Hillary, who reached the summit first. They
were mad because an Indian flag was included with the British and
Nepalese flags planted on the summit. In a society based on reason
such daring would find no sponsor. Yet, to me, the struggle makes a
statement about human nature. As you said, you can't separate intellect from emotion. Neither can you separate the cortex from the limbic system. Man has all the higher faculties you esteem, but he also has
animal instincts that make him endure and push him on.

Most people will say that myths are unreal, but that's not what the
Greeks, who invented the word, meant. Myth (muthos), mysticism
(mustikos), and mystery (musterion), are derived from musteion, to
close the eyes or the mouth. All three words are rooted in the experience of darkness and silence, which was a prerequisite for attaining
important kinds of knowledge. Yet the word myth today connotes
falsehood. Politicians dismiss reports of scurrilous activity by calling
them myths; scholars refer to mistaken views of the past as myths. A
detective story is called a mystery, and the essence of this genre is that
the problem must be solved.

I most like the writings of Claude Levi-Strauss, an anthropologist.
He doesn't look for the meaning of myth on the level of consciousness. Myth, for him, is an expression of primitive thought with a
purpose "to provide a logical model capable of overcoming contradiction." For him and me, the logic in mythical thought is as rigorous as
that of modern science. The difference lies not in the quality of that
intellectual process, but in the nature of things to which it is applied.

Does your foundation of reason exclude Mt. Everest? Who is the
arbiter of reason? How do you choose which reasons are true, and
which are false, except by your personal feelings and beliefs?

'I don't worry about which myths are true or false. I only need to
know what myths are beneficial and which are not. You can't prove
that any act of reasoning displays full and fundamental truth. All you

can show is that it presents a "logical model capable of overcoming contradiction." And that is all that myth, in the structuralist sense, does.

Did I tell you that I got a copy of the *Septuagint?* It is all Greek to me, but that doesn't mean I don't understand it! I love languages, and it is fascinating to see how the cultural mindset of a people is reflected in their forms of expression. Sigh! All this knowledge in the world, and even in a normal lifespan there is so little time to learn a little of it. How much more pressed am I, whose thread is short? I should have chosen the profession of janitor at a university so I could use its library without having to pay for it by producing scholarly treatises! Free knowledge just for pushing a broom! Wouldn't that be great? And I could hit on all the college chicks who studied late in the library. She says, "Go out with you? Why, you're nothing but a janitor!" Says I, "Right, but ask me how I got my nickname: Big Pee Wee." It would be a grand life. Then I'd quote Catullus to her in Latin: "Vivamus, Claudia, et Amamus!" And in no time flat her sycamores would be spread wide as the pillars of dawn! I might even shave my head and get an earring like Mr. Clean so I could polish the halls of female academia. It's not so bad a dream when you think about it. Spreading knowledge and . . . um . . . disseminating love. I'd press and starch my little gray uniform so as to cut a dashing figure of a janitor. Life would be good. I could start all kinds of heated arguments with any anthropologists who wandered into the library. Ah, what fun! All you have to do is let them declaim on a subject and, when they finish, just say, "Aw, bullshit!"

Two or three weeks left on the lockdown. Who knows what I'll think at that time. For now, though, I've trimmed the United Negro College Fund's slogan, "A mind is a terrible thing to waste" down to "A mind is a terrible thing."

Peace and Love to you and Zelda,
DW

April 22, 2001

Dear Charles,
Greetings! As always, it was good to hear from you, and many thanks for the $50.

You are perceptive—I was startled by your assertion that I was wrong. Not because I can't be wrong, but because such certitude in a matter which is unprovable is shocking to me.

Even the most liberal definition of knowledge convinces me that we rarely truly know anything, but rather mistake our opinions for essential truths.

Also shocking is this aspect. If you say, "I think you are wrong," or "I disagree," it is a premise for debate. It says that you take a contrary position, but when you say, "You're wrong," it is not an argument but a conclusion, which suggests that the debate is already over and that any opinion contrary to yours has been dismissed.

I admire your audacity, but it is shocking to witness directly. Owing to epistemic considerations and the inconclusive subject, neither you nor I can know the other is wrong. So, in so far as saying "You're wrong!" goes , well, Charles, you're wrong!

But Zelda is right. I've always been sensitive. My quest for meaning has led me to believe that all persons have worth and value. I want to respect them and be able to disagree without harming them. It's hard to do because I can be impassioned of opinion. But I try.

I just remembered something. If you think your "You're wrong" was shocking, you should have witnessed my flinches when my father would load up and fire a "Your ass sucks buttermilk!" version of "You're wrong." And that was when he was in a charitable humor!

Can I ask a big favor? My TV is on its last legs. I got it in 1989, and I surely got $159 worth of enjoyment from it. It is becoming unwatchable. The only TV we can buy here is a cheap, see-through plastic TV not half as good as one you could buy for half as much on the streets. It costs $199.99 (Why don't they just say $200? They're the only game in town.).

I look forward to the *New York Review of Books* subscription. Thanks for that.

> Hello and a hug for
> Zelda,
> DW

April 26, 2001

Dear DW,

I will get a postal money order for the TV when I mail this letter. I
am grateful that you let me know about this. It seems crazy that the
prison administration will let you buy a TV but not a typewriter.

You either misunderstood me, or decided to construct a straw man
from what I said about being demythologized and a rationalist. You
asked me why I was a Quaker, apparently realizing that I am not much
of a Christian. Since I don't remember ever believing Bible myths during my Presbyterian Sunday School education, I was demythologized
from the beginning. Those stories seemed to me to be as much fictions
as *The Little Engine Who Could* or the numerous Brer Rabbit stories
that I also heard.

Yet I am a Christian because, having grown up with these myths, I
respond to them in art, literature, and music. To find them aesthetically and morally valuable does not require that I believe they are true.
Somewhere in Jawaharlal Nehru's autobiography, *Toward Freedom,* he
compares the pantheon of Greek gods and their myths to the similarly
vast store of Hindu mythology to say how fortunate Europeans were
to have Greek mythology to enrich their civilization without having
to believe it. In contrast, he wrote that Hindu mythology weighs India
down with a great historical burden of religious superstition.

I joined the Quaker Meeting in Bloomington two years ago, despite
the fact that many Quakers believe Christian myths record actual historical events. I like the silent unprogrammed worship. The Meeting
gives me (Zelda does not attend) a community of more or less like
minded people.

A central Quaker notion is that each person has something they call
Spirit or the Inner Light. I avoid god-talk because it anthropomor-
phizes the divine, attributing human traits like justice, will, and love
to a divine personage. If you believe supernatural beings exist and intervene in human affairs you prejudge truth claims about them. Faith
precedes experience, interpreting it and determining its shape, but the
responsibility of critical intelligence is to unmask false beliefs, and to
erode blind faith (blind because it is immune to reason, and to percep-
tions of the world that are inconsistent with it). I think that the skeptical examination of one's faith, and of the faith of others, is essential to
civilization.

Of course, some kind of faith is essential, too. We act with limited
knowledge of what the consequences will be, or of why others and we

ourselves do what we do. My faith, unprovable but not unexamined, is that if there is something divine in each of us, it is our ability to reason. I have a broad conception of reason: some degree of reason can be observed in the cognitive and adaptive behavior of many animal species, but the human ability, grounded in grammatical language, is extraordinary. People may not reason very well, and reasoning is often distorted by self-interest. As a person matures his ability to observe the world accurately and to reason about it depends on the cultivation of feelings. An affectless person cannot learn; neither can a person with unruly emotions. Learning is achieved by training in manners, which cultivate emotions that facilitate the ability to observe and reason.

You write, "Owing to epistemic considerations and the inconclusive subject, neither you nor I can 'know' the other is 'wrong.'" If that is the case, argument is fruitless. Anything we say is merely a personal take on the subject, there are no standards external to our separate selves. Solipsism declares the end of intellectual exchange, and we are alone in touchy/feely worlds of our own making.

You write as if I did not know that there are poetic truths expressed in allegories, parables, myths, poems, and other works of art. Perception of these truths requires moral insight, creative imagination, and wisdom. These ways of knowing are indicated in a famous story about Isadora Duncan. When she was asked what one of her dances meant she said, "If I could tell you what it means I wouldn't have to dance it." That, I think, was a reasonable answer.

It is Saturday morning so I must end it and get to the post office before it closes.

Enjoy the new TV!
Charles

May 2, 2001

Dear Charles,

I received your letter and the TV money today—for both of which, thanks. Now I have to go through all sorts of administrative hoop-jumping to get the old TV out of my name so I can order a new one. Then I can only order on the last week of the month. If I miss this month, I have to wait until the end of the next. One has to take on an almost imploring manner which is quite distasteful. But that is part of prison ritual. Even the smallest things are morphed into ceremonies of the state's power over you. There is a sublime philosophical, or sociological, principle to it as reason is turned to a bad end. Just like myth, either can be beneficial, either can be evil. They are the two most perfect girlfriends: they'll let you do anything you want, as often as you like. The bad side, as humankind has all-too-often demonstrated, can absolutely prevail. Then myth and reason feed each other until the society does abundant evil and mythologizes it into smug virtue. So let us not love his own position too much in the coming discussion.

Let me stop here and define my thoughts and feelings concerning you. I sincerely believe that you are a good man who cares about people, but your education has been neglected in some areas, brother! I'm going to wait for a week or so to give your letter the meditation it deserves. I don't entirely disagree with you. I just have a more cynical slant on human nature.

I got my first copy of *The New York Review of Books* today. Thanks. It's a nice magazine, and all of a sudden William Blake is everywhere! I will look forward to this magazine's issues.

> Here's a hug for Zelda. Thanks for the TV money,
> DW

5

Knowledge

May 10, 200.

Dear Charles,

As advertised, I wanted to respond to some of your points. We are not in complete disagreement, I can tell you that right off. I didn' know how wide-ranging and how deep you intended for your state ment on "demythologizing" society to go. I took the logical extreme so you could back away from them according to your liking.

I can understand about your not being entirely satisfied with Chris tian myth. To my mind, good myths must fit the zeitgeist of the age If they don't, they become more and more useless.

One thing I would like to touch on briefly is your remark that peo ple may say one thing but act quite differently. I say it is good for people's reach to exceed their grasp. It is good that they set standard nobler than they themselves prove to be. Does this mean that we are animals with every animal instinct, and yet we are divine in having the need to be better than animals? Is this what you mean when you say (hedgingly) that if anything is divine in humankind it is the reason tha elevates us above our animal cousins?

I'm more expansive in what I consider to be divine. I think that sen tience, even down to the level of mere self-awareness and awarenes of the world is itself divine. Merely to be aware that you exist in thi vast universe of myriad existences is a "state of grace" in my mind. We humans are the pinnacle of this idea. But is there nothing divine o sacred about a fox vixen nursing her kits?

I take your point about how Hindu mythology was thought by Nehru to weigh India down with a great historical burden of supersti tion. If myth weighs down on a people more than it uplifts them, then it's time for new myths. You must be saying, why do we need myths at all? Why can't we all just do the reasonable thing? Why indeed. There is something about human minds that needs a story. The un

84

known is a terrible thing. Maybe that is why we insist on having stories about who we are, where we came from, and why we are here. Now maybe you ask, "What's wrong with the real story that science has fairly well demonstrated to this point?" Well, it just ain't sexy enough. It gives no passion. You have to be a fire-breathing god to impress me. I can argue with any man, but an all-knowing God must know more than me. So we need a story.

When I was young I believed in science. I believed in the big bang, evolution, and so forth. I believed in consequence that nothing really mattered. We were here by fluke, to begin with. I didn't even know my great-grandparents' names, or if they were good or bad people. They were swallowed up in the yawning maw of Time, and it made no difference what they were like. Man would go on and on and do all these things, and then the sun would swell up and burn everything, and none of it would matter to the universe. That hit me when I was about ten years old and made me profoundly depressed. I don't matter, you don't matter, mankind is an accidental and irrelevant gas ball in the intestines of the universe. We'd dissipate like farts in the wind. It was terrible. I thought of killing myself many times. Finally, I just said, "To hell with it. I'll do whatever I want." And I did.

I had no story to give me a significant place in the universe. So I blew where the winds carried me and just did whatever the situation called for when I got there. Myth is the Cartesian grid upon which we plot our fine algebra. Without it, there is only a terrible despair and emptiness and certain knowledge that not a single thing that people do makes any difference. The outcome is set and final, and all that humans do will be swept away. The wise man and the fool end up in the grave in no particular order. If you don't let me have a story, why should I be good?

In any case, are there "objective standards for judging what is true or false, correct or incorrect, beautiful or ugly, moral or immoral?" Maybe, but they are mostly subjective and personal. I am not saying that every single thing we believe is mere opinion. For example, because we agree to an arbitrary system of measurement we can be certain that a given object is $6'' \times 3'' \times 2''$. We can agree that the sun appears to rise in the east, even when it actually doesn't rise at all, but the face of the globe turns to it. We can have all sorts of practical beliefs that are true enough for our purposes. But there is never an end to the argument of how many angels can dance on the head of a pin, assuming that angels exist and that they're disposed to dance on pinheads. We can't go back now and say whether early humans had male hunters and female gatherers, or whether something else entirely went on. We can only look at artifacts and conjecture; we can only look at present-day humans and theorize. Inasmuch as every man peers out through the filter of his own mind, things will look quite different to different people. If my whole life has been spent in the desert, I can't conceive of a marsh. If you spent your life in a marsh, you can't conceive of the desert. We all think we can educate ourselves enough to see the world "as it really is." But we see it as we see it, god help us. You and I can never touch upon the knowledge of what it is like to be black or Cro-Magnon. I can tell you how both appear in the desert, and you may have some insight into them from the marsh. In the end we can never know, even though we have one people right here with us. We know what we know, but never know what we don't know.

Well, I just took a break to fix a couple of tuna salad sandwiches. They were very good. They had liver for supper, and I can't eat that stuff. So it was nice to have some tuna on the shelf. I have to say, the quality of my life has much improved since I met you. Formerly I would have just gone hungry. If I seem to suffer overmuch (or at least go on about my existential angst), take what cheer you can in that you relieve me of some of it with your coin.

I've ranted enough for one letter. Here's a hug for Zelda, and my hope that my letter has been entertaining enough to make you want to respond.

Until next time,
DW

June 12, 2001

Dear DW,

I have been meaning to write, but somehow the days go by and I don't do what I intend to do. I will drive up to see you soon. I haven't written because we took off to visit my brother and his wife in Little Rock. He is 87 and his son phoned to tell us that he is close to death.

We visited Evansville on the way to Arkansas to see if I could consult the *Evansville Courier* files to read about you. At the reception desk in the newspaper lobby the clerk remembered you and wise-cracked, "He wiped out a whole family, and now he is studying law at the taxpayer's expense." I missed her sarcasm, and, puzzled, said, "He's studying law? That's strange; he never told me that he was studying law. I have been visiting and corresponding with him. He never told me about that." Later I thought my response was better than it would have been if I had understood her. The *Courier* files are on microfilm in the Evansville public library. I also found them in the university library in Bloomington. I have read the January 16th issue, when you made the front page. I will have to go back to read more.

Perhaps I have seen too many crime movies, but you were not the least bit clever. The newspaper story made me think that you wanted to be caught. The police immediately suspected that it was your crime! You had been arrested for robbing another house in the area, and you were out on bail. Your signature was all over the place. At the victims' house and the one next door you taped windows before breaking them in exactly the same way you had done in the earlier robbery. After the murders, rather than changing your appearance, assuming a new identity, and getting out of town fast, you hung around where you were bound to be caught. In childhood you were repeatedly caught when you ran away from reform schools and engaged in petty theft. Would you say now that your behavior was deliberately self-defeating? Is there anything to the notion that you wanted to be punished?

A common idea is that young people who get caught breaking rules may want to be punished for other things that they have gotten away with. Guilt feelings often motivate our actions. Could that explain why when you were a boy you were so frequently caught, and after the murders so easily identified and caught?

Last Tuesday at the local prison I talked at length to two boys, 16 or 17 years old, who were arrested in Evansville for a bank robbery in Bloomington. They escaped with the money, but an accomplice who got caught identified them to the police. They were arrested with the loot and brought back to Bloomington. One of the boys said that he had been in reform school from age 13. The other said that he had dropped out of school and his parents had tried to get him not to hang out with his buddy because he was a bad influence. Finally, his father kicked him out of the house. His father refused phone calls from prison, but his mother took them if he called her at the beauty shop where she worked. They had been stealing to buy drugs and had arrest records for that.

It was sad to see them throwing their lives away. I and the Quaker woman I go to the prison with did not preach to them. We listened in a neutral but friendly manner. I thought of you at that age. Wasn't your family also in Mt. Vernon? The newspaper said the police had been looking for you there immediately after your crime was discovered.

Evansville is farther from Bloomington than I thought when I offered to bring some member of your family with me to Michigan City. If you had taken me up on the offer I would not have been able to do it without spending a night in Michigan City, and perhaps one in Evansville.

Yours truly,
Charles

June 14, 2001

Dear Charles,

Hi. I hope this letter finds you and Zelda in good spirits and health. I haven't heard from you in awhile, so I hope all is okay with you.

I ordered the new TV on May 31st. They bring around a sheet every Wednesday that shows how much money we have on our accounts. On the 6th the $199.99 was gone from mine. Opinions vary from two weeks to a month as to when I'll get the TV. At least, I know it's on the way. Again, thank you.

They killed Tim McVeigh. The article on the motives for executions in the latest *New York Review of Books* was right on point. Nietzsche was a nut sometimes, but occasionally he excelled, especially when examining morality and its motives. He said that we live in a society discouraged from thinking and encouraged to emote. Thinking people have problems with death penalty rationalizations. Emotional people find flawless sense in Bush's characterization of an execution as "Not vengeance, but justice."

They're supposed to kill a guy here on June 27. I dislike him intensely. He's a snitch and a collaborator, and he's done evil to me personally. But I don't want them to kill him. He had a clemency hearing today. Clemency is usually pro forma, a show of pretended solemn deliberation. A prison official testified that they can't run prisons without snitches like Lowery, so maybe he'll catch a break.

Well, enough for now.

Your friend,
DW

Tuesday, June 19, 2001

Dear DW,

Your June 14th letter arrived yesterday. Our letters must have crossed in the mail.

The May 7 *Newsweek* article "Religion and the Brain" that you sent me is a splendid example of bad science. It happens this way: brain imaging technology was invented, driven by the need to diagnose tumors and other disorders. Large amounts of funding are available for brain research. Some psychologists decide to see if people have "criminal brains" or "homosexual brains." They get hundreds of thousands of dollars to take pictures of brains of prisoners and homosexuals. Guess what? They find what they are looking for! Likewise, some psychologists are Christian believers, and they get large grants to use this expensive machinery to find religion in the brain. Meanwhile their deans and department chairman are impressed by the size of the grants, and the publicity in magazines, and on TV talk shows. The scientists get promotions and invited to Europe or Japan for international conferences.

The journalist who wrote the *Newsweek* article, and the psychologists she consulted, claimed that "despite its centrality to the mental lives of so many people, religion has been met by what David Wulff calls indifference or even apathy on the part of science." Well, one of your favorite authors, and a founder of academic psychology was William James, and one of his most important books was *The Varieties of Religious Experience*. It has been in print for over 100 years. I wonder if that Christian psychology professor, or the journalist, ever heard of Freud's *Totem and Taboo*, or Max Weber's *The Protestant Ethic and the Spirit of Capitalism*, or Tawney's *Religion and the Rise of Capitalism*. Anthropologists have made natural science studies of religions in many different cultures for well over a century. It is a central topic in our discipline and among sociologists. The claim that science has neglected research on religion only shows the abysmal ignorance of the person who made it.

As evidence for the assertion that scientists have neglected research on religion, Newsweek says, "When one psychologist, a practicing Christian, tried to discuss in his introductory psych *(sic)* book the role of faith in people's lives, his publisher edited out most of it. . . . The rise of neurotheology represents a radical shift in that attitude." Neurotheology? What a bastard that theology must be! Unless, of course, it is Christian, like that psychology textbook writer. But then what part of Christian dogma does brain imaging support? The virgin birth? Walking on water? Do you really want to claim that this "science" supports your "hard wiring" theory of the human condition?

You write that you "believed in science . . . in the big bang, evolution, and so forth when you were 10 years old, and reasoned in consequence that nothing really mattered. We were here by fluke." You were a precocious child. When I consider what the schools and other institutions were like in that part of Indiana, and the probable social class and family culture in which you grew up, I find that an improbable account of your childhood belief. How much science did you know when you were ten years old? The children one hears about who do very well in their science courses in school are elated by the subjects and proud of their accomplishments. The only notion I had as a child was that science was "hard," involving a lot of math, which I was not good at, so I avoided science courses in high school. I don't recall anything being identified as science before the 9th grade. Thus, I never learned any science through systematic instruction and study before I got to college.

You assert that when you were ten years old your understanding of scientific theories caused you to think that "mankind is an accidental and irrelevant gas ball in the intestines of the universe." To me this sounds like the anti-scientific stereotype of fundamentalist Christian sects that appeals primarily to uneducated or poorly educated people. Among these people the Bible is held to give a literal historical account of how the world was created. The cosmology derived from modern physics and astronomy, and scientific research on evolution are said to deprive the world of meaning, and to undermine morality. Well, I can believe that those ideas were part of the culture of southern Indiana that you grew up in. I can understand from other things you have told me about your childhood that you were depressed, but I can't believe that it was because you understood anything about modern science when you were ten years old.

I put your hunger for mythic accounts of the world as part of your romanticism. Myths are entertaining and aesthetically instructive. We can respond to their pleasing mysteries, their ambiguities, their wit, their symmetry. But I, for one, respond better by taking them as fictions, and in a world of modern science and high technology, I fear people who literally believe them. When scientific knowledge is available to us we are responsible to know some of it, and to respect the communities that cultivate such knowledge. Our tolerance of antiscientific attitudes has to be limited by recognition of dangers they pose to the larger society. For example, the danger of the Bush administration's failure to appoint a science adviser to the president, and its flouting of large bodies of informed scientific opinion about stem cell research, antiballistic missile technology, or global warming, or, to go back a way, Mrs. Reagan consulting an astrologer to decide how her husband should schedule presidential activities. To have such people in power is not funny, it is dangerous.

Whether you or I have brains hard wired to believe that powerful gods, or a single God, guide or guides our destinies, doesn't make a difference for anyone other than you and me. So there is nothing between us to be intolerant about. Still, that term, *hard wired*, sets me off.

You write, "Myth is the Cartesian grid upon which we plot our fine algebra. Without it, there is only a terrible despair and emptiness, and certain knowledge that not a single damned thing that people do makes any difference." This sounds very fine, but is really very foolish. Why can't I use reason and empirical observation to try to see human life at it is; its cruelty, ugliness, kindness, and beauty? And, then, rather than surrendering to emptiness and despair because there is so much suffering in the world, why shouldn't I enjoy the good things that come my way while trying, somehow, to use reason and empirical knowledge to improve my own circumstances and circumstances of others? Why does finding ancient and medieval myths unbelievable deprive the world of hope and meaning? You find the stuff liberating, but it would suffocate me.

I would rather have had the liver than the canned tuna sandwiches, depending, of course, on whether it was very fresh liver, properly cooked with sweet onions, butter, and Marsala wine. Don't break my ankles for that remark. I will visit you day after tomorrow, before you get this letter.

Peace,
Charles

June 20, 2001

Dear Charles,
Hi. Got your letter yesterday. I hope your brother gets better. I guess we prepare slowly but surely for the day when we won't get bet-

ter. I used to think that life must taste flatter as you aged. Now I think it tastes sweeter in direct ratio to your awareness of your own mortality.

It would be easy if your conclusions were conclusive: that I was not clever because I wanted to be caught and punished. The reason I wasn't clever was that I was a drooling dope fiend before I entered that house. I had no center. The only constant in my life was a gnawing pain which flared into acute despair at times. I medicated this condition with all the drugs I could pump into my veins. I looked ahead and saw no future. I looked behind and saw a meaningless past. I was unloved even by my own parents. So I shot dope all day and had to steal all night to pay for it. After eight full weeks of this I was haggard. I was shooting about two grams of MDA, a gram of methamphetamine, and about 500 mg of Talwin every day. I would also do coke, LSD, PCP, hash, weed, and whatever presented itself on a given day. Sometimes I was hoping I'd just OD and get it over with. I knew I would eventually in any case.

By the day of the murders, 14 January 1980, I was a walking husk, carrying out almost autonomous functions to maintain the pattern of my life. Charles, picture yourself standing over four dead bodies with a smoking gun in your hand. If you can think two "clever" thoughts, you're one cold-blooded mother-fucker. I was capable only of perfunctory TV movie of the week attempts to conceal what I'd done. My mind was shattered. I just fumbled around stupidly, occasionally thinking of what someone in my position might do about it. There was no "release" of all my pent up pain. It just magnified and multiplied until I literally wanted to jump out of my skin. I was so sick so deep in my soul that "cleverness" was meaningless.

I did not want to be caught and punished. In fact, even though I'd been escaping, or trying to, all my life, never had I so acutely felt a need to escape. I desperately wanted to escape. But I was overwhelmed by the horrible death frieze engraved on my mind. So I flailed about like a drowning man looking for purchase of any sort. There was none to be found. I couldn't summon a single clever idea. I did not want to go back to prison. I tried to stumble away as best I could, and that wasn't very good.

I don't know what answers to what questions you seek. I did it. The I who did it is not the I who writes this. Do you look for some event in my life that "caused" this? Too simple, my friend. It took 22 years to get there. You will not find a way to sum it up in a sentence or paragraph or chapter or book. Events surely affect us. There are paths and choices. At each fork in the road you choose, and the roads aren't marked. If you make enough bad choices you come into a land where it no longer matters which fork you take. One does create a very real Karmic field around oneself. If you keep adding to it, without ameliorating it, it will certainly collapse on you sooner or later.

The newspapers and courts will tell you nothing about these things because neither one is truly concerned with them. You said that you sometimes wondered why your life turned out so well. If I read secondhand reports about you, would I be able to explain your life accurately? Could I produce any one or several causes for your good fortune? I could posit causes, but you would likely be astonished at how wrong or oversimplified my conclusions were. You once wrote that you could not explain your own life. Think of me sitting in cells for 21 and a half years thinking about all this. How many volumes of books would 21 and a half years of thoughts fill? And each one led to the next, and each aggregate of them paved the way for the next aggregate. You can't leave them out any more than a scientist can skip over equations of fluid dynamics and get accurate results.

There are no excuses for what I did. There are no easy explanations.

There's a scientific explanation for why lightning strikes, and no doubt one could present a million-termed equation of why it struck in one precise time and place if one could know every single factor involved. But one doesn't and probably never will be able to. It has to suffice that we know that darkening skies and rumbling thunder mean lightning is likely to strike somewhere around us. There isn't much we can do about it. It is the same with people.

I know you think the world can be fixed. You think if you could identify key factors in my life you could intervene successfully in future lives. I think the weather has fewer variables than the human zeitgeist and any one pinpoint in its 5 plus billion fold ever changing loci. Either God has a plan for our perfection or whatever accident that created us will move us to an equally accidental conclusion. Either way, there's not much we can do outside the scope of our own actions, which are equally either part of God's plan, or accidental.

Sorry to be so pessimistic. These are my true feelings. I don't know if it's God or an accident. God gives hope, accident only gives chance. I realized at age 10, though, that one day the sun will turn angry red and devour the world. I sought refuge in science-fiction tales of interstellar colonization and exploration, but it's not much more consoling than any other escape.

Well, what the hell, maybe it could be worse!

> Your friend,
> DW

June 22, 2001

Dear Charles,

Thank you for the letter which came today. I enjoyed our visit, but regretted that we couldn't continue our discussion a little longer.

I now see what you were talking about when you made some points about "junk science." Your critique of the article on brain imaging made not a single point about the science itself. You only attacked the journalistic effort to report it. That doesn't invalidate the science. You use the article as a "fine example of junk science," whereas I see it as an imperfect report of science which may be valid. Our approach seems distinctly different. I employ Occam's razor. You seem to apply a political standard of possible consequences in determining whether any scientific statement is good or junk.

Okay, the journalist committed a grievous crime in using the popular term "psych" rather than psychology. The other error she made which seemed to get your goat was her assertion that science eschewed any study of religion. She may think only the physical sciences are science, and not the subjective sciences like sociology, psychology, philosophy, anthropology. I think they are sciences, but the vulgar (in the Latin sense of "common") do not ordinarily think of subjective sciences when they think of scientists. To slam her for this is merely to employ the hackneyed debate tactic of *falsus in unus, falsus in omnibus*, false in one point, false in all of them.

Now, as to what I knew and when I knew it. I was an odd child. Kids of my age group seemed infantile to me. I tried hanging out with older kids, but I found their intelligene wanting and my cheerful willingness to point this out to them netted several ass whippings. I was lonely and alienated. During all but the winter months of '67 and '68 I practically lived in the Willard Library, which you recently visited. Books became my best friends. They offered an escape for my loneliness. I was fascinated by books themselves. The smell of them. The look and feel of them. And, of course, what strange and wonderful things they said to me. I read the entire Encyclopedia Britannica, every word in it. I can't remember a thousandth of them, but I read them! I learned all kinds of things that only seemed to amuse me and no one else. For example, I could look up the declination and right ascension of any celestial body, calculate true local time from GMT, point to a place on the ceiling of my room and say, "Arcturus is right there!" Then I would run outside and look, and sure enough, Arcturus was precisely where I predicted. This fascinated me and thrilled me no end. When I was interrogated about why I was running in and out of the house at all hours of the night and I explained it, my father said, "That's the stupidest thing I've ever heard in my life!" But I already hated him, so I dismissed him as the buffoon that he was.

You haven't been to school in awhile. The Big Bang was 3rd grade science in my day. Geometry came in the fourth grade. Introductory algebra began at the end of the 5th grade. I was 10 when I started the 5th grade in 1968, but I had already learned considerably more than the 5th grade could teach. I clowned in class and got all F's and D's. I was never recognized as anything special except for being especially a pain in their ass. I spent more time in the corner, or the hall, or in the principal's office than I did in class. I was very sullen and hostile. I would do irritating shit like correct a teacher's grammar when she misspoke. I'm sure you can imagine how beloved I was. I was a smart-ass little kid with a chip on his shoulder.

It was not any leap of genius to figure out that nothing mattered. The universe had a genesis. It will certainly have an end. Our sun was only 4 billion years old. Eventually it would burn off all its hydrogen and begin to burn mostly helium, a lighter element. Having lost its mass, its gravity would not compress it as before, and it would turn a sullen red and expand to enormous proportions, to where its surface would expand past the orbit of earth. The earth and everything on it would be incinerated. That would be the end of humanity. It's elementary science. No matter to what stupefying heights of perfection human kind might rise, it and all its works would be swallowed by an angry sun, and that would be that. There was no escape from this fate. I learned that our sun was small and not very bright. If you traveled a mere 60 light years away and turned around to look back, you would not see it with your naked eye. Sixty light years makes not even a speck in the universe. We were on a little ball of dirt orbiting a tiny sun in a little galaxy among countless galaxies spanning distances that are incomprehensible to a human mind.

Even if we learned interstellar travel and left our sun, the universe itself would still finally succumb to the second law of thermodynamics, which I well knew of from reading sci-fi since I was about seven. Still, the end of everything was as if we had never been. You seem to doubt what I know now, or what I knew then. It makes no difference. In a hundred years who will know that you doubted? No one will remember that I existed at all. I began to see that everything was meaningless. All the things people thought were important were just pastimes in a vagrant corner of the great universe. They meant nothing. Whether you believe I knew this or not, it sent me reeling. It changed everything. It raised the pitch of my despair.

My time in the library was to seek refuge from the loveless, meaningless mess of my own personal existence. Somehow I came to think that if I expanded my point of view widely enough, then I could surpass my own circumstances and find a haven in being superior to my problems. So I expanded my outlook with a vengeance only to find that in the end the universe gave less a damn about me than my own family. And my family didn't give a damn about me at all.

It was all downhill from there. Punishments didn't matter: I simply could not be any more miserable than I already was. I did whatever I wanted whenever I wanted to do it. I seemed to dare greatly to others. I just didn't give a fuck. It's not daring to face something that means nothing to you. This world had, and still has, no punishments greater than the misery I felt most of my life.

Here is a thing you do: "Well, I can believe that those ideas were a part of the culture of southern Indiana where you grew up." This implies that my ignorance is not my fault, but that I was contaminated by the culture of southern Indiana. It is identical as saying to a black person, "I can understand how your negritude prevents you from understanding what I, in my magnificent alabasterness know to be the plain truth." It is arrogant and biased. You love science; therefore science cannot be blamed for my despair. I never said that science gave me despair. It was the realization that there was no escape from my despair.

You are probably right: I am a solipsist and a romantic, if darkly so. I assert my right to be this merely by right of being it. Life is what we make it. People understand this to mean that you get out of life what you put into it, in a sort of karmic sense. Yet I mean it literally. Outside the obvious physical truths, such as "rock is hard" and "falling more than 50 feet will probably kill you," the world is what each of us believes it to be. As much as each of us is unique, we are wrong; and as much as we are all the same, we are right. We never know exactly where and when we are wrong, so I make it up as I go along. I build an edifice that uplifts me. That makes me tolerate others. That makes me think being good is rewarded, and being evil is punished. It makes me see that life is wonderful and terrible and that, on the whole, I like existing and recommend it to all.

I take myths as fictions just like you do. I take them as fictions typifying universal themes. Why are we responsible to know some of science when it is available to us? Why respect communities that cultivate it? I agree, but what edict has been proclaimed on such and by whom?

If you say it is "reasonable" that we should, I'll leave you alone. But can a myth maker assert the same privilege for what he holds dear and most important? You mention in the same paragraph Bush's failure to appoint a science advisor and his flouting of informed opinion about anti-ballistic missile technology. I don't want to sound like a religious reactionary, but where the hell did ballistic missiles come from in the first place? Southern Indiana? Science is great and has given us many marvels. It has also created some of the most diabolical devices the mind could conceive. Poisons, gunpowder, bombs, rockets, spy satellites, and a host of other evils can be laid at the door of scientists.

You say that "our tolerance of antiscientific attitudes has to be limited by recognition of dangers they pose to the larger society." Couldn't someone say, with equal gravity and concern that "our tolerance of scientific research has to be limited by recognition of dangers it poses to larger society." If this were the prevailing ethic, then there would be no ballistic missiles with nuclear warheads to cause someone else to think of a defense against them. Because scientists think they are supreme arbiters, they resist being limited by negritude in the face of their alabasterness. We have DDT, and nitrates fucking up the soil and waters, and fuel additives, and thalidomide babies, and nuclear waste and toxic wastes and solvents in the ground water, and space junk, and unexploded landmines, and weapons of mass destruction, and on and on. Scientists gave us those things, not people at prayer. Not makers of myth.

Don't get me wrong: I see the terrible ravages that myths gone awry have wrought on the world, but until the advent of modern science, their range was limited. Science gives them the power to destroy the whole world. In the words of the blues singer, "Before you accuse me, take a look at yourself."

I like science because knowledge of any sort intrigues me. I like myth because it can give a context to my operant reasoning. I can't see a single thing that makes either one of them superior to the other.

This rant has gone long enough. I really enjoyed it, though. May you be well and happy, and may the rituals of your life be propitious before the gods, under whatever form you disguise them. (That's really low of me to lay a barb even in what was otherwise a sincere wish for your well-being, but I'm just insufferable like that sometimes.)

Hi to Zelda, and hope to see you again soon.

Until next time,
DW

June 28, 2001

Dear DW,

A brief note. My brother died peacefully on the 26th, and the funeral is tomorrow.

I enjoyed our visit last week and your letter when we returned to Bloomington. Plus the very long letter a few days later. You are a skilled polemicist, but, dear friend, you argue in circles. You misunderstand me most of the time. I don't know why because I am always lucid as well as concise.

I will write at greater length when we return from Arkansas.

Best,
Charles

June 28, 2001

Dear Charles,

Just want to let you know that I got my TV on Monday. It's so nice to have a clear picture. Thanks again.

As I'm sure you know, they killed Jim Lowery after midnight on Tuesday. Someone told me that they had the largest protest outside since Gregory Resnover's execution in 1994. You would never have known it by the media here. Not a single report on TV until Tuesday night at 10, and then about a 20-second story.

Hope you enjoyed my provocative rant in the last letter.

Peace,
DW

July 11. 2001

Dear Charles,

Hi. I received your card and the money order today, for which thanks. Yes, I am guilty! I exaggerate your position for the sake of my polemics. Was Hamlet's fortune really outrageous in its slings and arrows? Or did it just add a little dramatic flair to his soliloquy to so characterize it? When a dog gets hold of a sock does it really need to shake its head all about as if bringing down serious prey? Or is such gusto part of the fun of being a dog that caught a sock? Quien sabe? All I know is that when I get a sock in my teeth I whip it all around as if it were the veriest buffalo to feed the pups in the den. And even if I growl fiercely and bare fangs in the midst of it, just look at my tail. It's wagging in undisguised glee.

See here, good fellow, accusing me of arguing in circles will get you nowhere. In fact, if I commit any of the ten fallacies of logic, it is that of ignoratio elenchi I never argue in circles. I argue in irregular polyhedrons, and those derive from the sphere, not the circle. The problem is obvious: you were confined to the plane of 2-D thinking, seeing circles everywhere, when I was on the 3-D plane of spheres. See, it's bad to argue in circles, but it's good to argue in spheres.

I've been enjoying my new TV, but it is annoying, too. It used to be that everything on TVs was adjusted with a knob dedicated to that function. Now everything is electronic. You punch "Menu" and your channel selector buttons, Volume $+/-$ controls, Double, Triple, Quadruple, and so on for other things. I miss knobs. Worse, this TV won't even try to bring in a bad station. At the slightest loss of signal it throws up its hands in defeat and goes blue screen. It doesn't even try. I liked TVs you could pound on and coax and cajole into doing better shows.

I do like this closed caption stuff, though. I like to have a TV picture on while listening to the radio. With closed captioning I can hear the radio and read the TV.

The V-chip seems like a childish device to me. It absolves and relieves responsibility from immature and lazy parents. Down with it!

Yours,
DW

6

Science Itself

Dear Charles,

Your pronouncement on the "junkiness" of brain imaging troubled me greatly. I couldn't get to sleep easily for many nights. I tend to obsess on things I don't understand, worrying them all about until they make some sort of sense. If you could dismiss the preliminary conclusions of scientists without even having to examine their data, why couldn't I? What could you see that was invisible to me? Was I dense? Unschooled? Very annoying stuff. Finally my thinking turned to science itself. I began to wonder if there was a paradigm for the scientific process itself. If so, how would it work?

I'm enclosing a flow chart which greatly comforts me, giving exact coordinates for even your prediction of "junkiness" as a part of the whole. I sleep much better now. It makes perfect sense to me, restores order to my concept of science. But, does it bear any relation to the real world of science? Does it omit any vital processes? Does it add unnecessary processes? Can there even be such a simple and universal diagram of the processes of science relating to the individual scientists and the collective traditions of science?

After all my tossing and turning, this seemed too simple a solution. Still, it's comforting. Is it fact or myth? The little atomic model of a nucleus with electrons whirling around it is not at all what an atom "looks" like. Most people don't know that this popular bit of "science" is in fact "myth." It's just a convenient model to symbolize the atom. How often, brother, is science mythical and myth scientific?

Yours,
DW

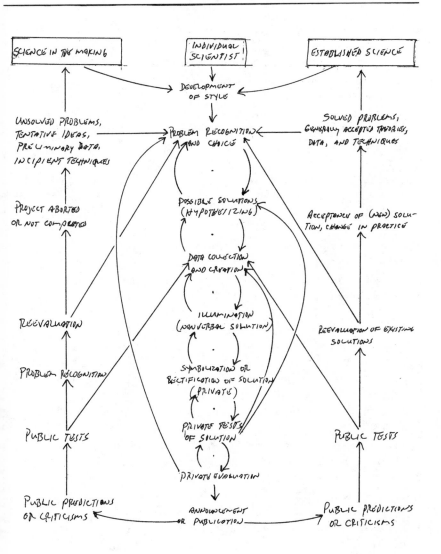

6. Science itself.

July 22, 2001

Dear DW,

Glad to hear that you have liberal sentiments about censorship and the V-chip. I doubt that you have seen the hard-core pornography that some cable companies broadcast, or even the soft-core nudity and simulated sexual intercourse occasionally on Home Box Office and some other channels. I would not have wanted our children to see that stuff until they were well into their teens.

Your angst as a child about the end of the world reminded me that I, too, in childhood thought about the cosmos. I once made myself dizzy trying to imagine that everything that I was looking at was even less than a speck of dust in a vast expanse of space. I repeated the thought experiment many times. The curious thing is that I took pleasure in the effort of cosmic imagination, while your cosmological imagination confirmed your despair. So, yes, I credit your claim to a fuck-it attitude, the world will end in fire anyway. But I don't think this has anything to do with scientific knowledge.

You should not have been upset by my remark about junk science. Look at the context. All I said was that the quality of scientific work is variable, and much misguided work is driven by the personal ambition of scientists and the availability of funding. I did not say that all research using the new technology of imaging the brain was junk science, but a lot of it is. How would I know? You sent me a perfect example: a scientist who advocates something called "neurotheology." He is a Christian who studies religious sentiments supposedly reflected in brain images.

Your model for how scientific knowledge is created is admirable for the comprehensive way you reflected on the subject. A chart of this kind is too abstract for me. As a teacher I preferred to reason inductively from particular historical case material. In a course called Magic, Science, and Religion I selected materials we would conventionally identify as belonging to one or another to these cultural domains. We began with an ethnological study of an epidemic of Kuru in New Guinea. Kuru was a 100 percent fatal illness that affected an isolated population. In research that led to a Nobel Prize, it was attributed to a "slow virus" (later, to a prion). However, local people understood the illnesses as an affliction caused by sorcery. Both scientists and the local people assumed an orderly universe of cause and effect relationships that could be observed, and inferences from observations could be empirically tested. Both assumed that knowledge gained in this manner might enhance their power to intervene and change the course of the illness. The difference was that the observations and reasoning of foreign scientists and New Guinea natives were grounded in different institutional networks and historical bodies of cultural knowledge.

From that opening discussion we would go on to other cases: a 17th-century Catholic Church document on how to investigate witches and conduct witchcraft trials; Harvey's treatise on the circulation of blood (widely considered a perfect illustration of "scientific method"); a book by journalists on scientific fraud discovered in research conducted at distinguished American universities; an ethnological study of different forms of Islamic religion in Morocco and Java that raised the issue of the generic character of religion. Discussions of this diverse case material would show that the domains of religion, magic, and science, are polytypical, and overlap each other in particular times and places. We use the terms magic, science and religion to identify different historical complexes of social action that we sort out by recognizing "family resemblances." You will, of course, recognize this concept borrowed from Wittgenstein.

A widespread opinion among scientists and historians is that there are various ways of "doing science," and these variations are located in communities of workers who have conventional ways of evaluating each other's work. These conventions are their science, and like other social conventions they change. One view of this was that the changes are progressive and have been continuous since the Scientific Revolution of the 17th century. Kuhn disagreed and identified what he called revolutionary "paradigm shifts" in different subjects of scientific study (astronomy, physics, chemistry, etc.). Between shifts he called work that assumes a paradigm "normal science." Normal science simply fills in the blank spaces created by the paradigm.

Sincerely,
Charles

September 3, 2001

Dear Charles,
Today is my 44th birthday. I'm really surprised to still be alive. Did you see the July 25 *Indianapolis Star* article about me? They

really roasted me. The title was "Killer who took 4 lives 21 years ago
still has his." They had pictures of the 4 victims, and then a big super-
imposed print of the angriest mug shot I ever took here. Since I've had
more than 15 mug shots taken since I've been here, the selection was
obviously deliberate. I look like I'm poised to jump off the page and
murder someone on the spot. Don't get me wrong. I think the victims'
survivors are entitled to their feelings, and I understand their frustration.

The death penalty actually leaves people feeling like they've been
cheated, or that "justice" has been delayed. If there were no death
penalty, and if I'd gotten a sentence of life without parole from the
get-go, then no one would be upset now. Justice would have long been
meted out, and everyone could have gotten on with their lives. When
I first was arrested, I was offered a plea-bargain. If I would plead guilty
right then, they wouldn't ask for the death penalty, and I would have
received a 240-year sentence (of which I'd have to serve no less than
120 years). If I had taken that deal, justice would not be "on hold" as
people think it is now. I've suffered harder than I would have if I had
taken the deal. Because the sentence is death, the time counts for
nothing, and people think I'm laughing behind my hand about it all.

We end up in the same place, you and I, of choosing what we want
to believe. You do it by judging the science "sound" or "junk." I do it
by accepting all scientific truths, but if I don't like the results, I just
ignore them. I do believe there is such a thing as "junk science," like
William Reich's "Orgone." The great cause of junk science is "scien-
tism," the belief that science answers to all problems. Since science
has been exalted to such a state of authority, everyone wants to use it
to justify his personal views, or to delegitimatize someone else's views.

"Love at first sight" has been proven again and again, and never
disproved, to be neurochemical. But I am a poet, so love at first sight
is a universe of possibilities to me—a million metaphors. "O Thou
intoxicating Vision of Beauty, fair as ten jeweled virgins dancing about
the hermit moon; I swear to Thee by the peridot flagons of spring, to
quaff to the dregs Thy chalice of Glory, and beget a royal race before
the Dawn flees from awakening Day!"

Tell me, brother, what candle does science hold to that ecstatic
flame? I accept science as a form of or an aspect of truth, but I will
never let it dictate the meaning of my existence. I think you do the
same as I, but you try to salvage your high regard for science by finding ways to discredit science you don't personally like. As for me, these
two things are equally beautiful: (1) $E = mc2$ and (2) "O Thou Eter-

nal river of chaotic law, in whose depths lie locked the secrets of creation; I swear to Thee by primal waters of the Deep, to suck up the Firmament of Thy Chaos, and as a volcano to belch forth a Cosmos coruscating suns." The first is valid in one field of operation, the second is valid in another.

I apologize if my thinking sometimes seems perverse and rambling. Maybe it is indefensible, but I have worked long and hard to come to this place of seeing with the mind and feeling with the heart at once; of believing that there must be One All-Inclusive Truth which admits of no contradiction, but that such a truth is beyond the ken of humans, and therefore no single human field or ideology can explain it, or provide the One Way of human thinking, or existence. It was hard to get here: extremely difficult to hold opposites in each hand and to see that they were the same.

But I am also high today, and once again the scourge of drugs may have struck down what would otherwise have been a sensible conversation. I certainly had fun, even if it proves to have been all nonsense! I just love to rant and to lapse into orgiastic poetry.

I should call it a day. I have the urge to lie down in self-sacrifice to the diabolical TV and eat large amounts of pretzels dipped in jalapeño cheese dip. Oh how depraved the acts cannabis inspires in its tragic victims!

I hope Zelda is doing better. Until next time.

DW

October 3, 2001

Dear DW,

I have thought often of writing, but Zelda was ill so I have shopped and done housework. We both have been preoccupied by the move to our new apartment. We had the closing on September 7 and started at once to take things over in our car. This involved a lot of walking and I damaged my foot, which then got infected. I doubled my daily intake of an antibiotic without stopping the infection, so I doubled that and finally realized I had a resistant strain of some kind.

The rotten part is that this has kept me off my feet so that I have been no use in setting up house in the new place. We had the help of my son and his wife, and two friends who painted walls, fixed track lights for our paintings, and so on. The main part of our move was scheduled for September 11, and despite the horrible destruction of the World Trade Center we went ahead with it.

When I was a professor at NYU we lived on the 20th floor of an apartment building with bedroom windows facing the Wall Street district. We watched the World Trade Center being built from the ground up. On Sundays my son and I would bicycle down to explore the area. At that time there were almost no residential buildings on that side of lower Manhattan. Chinatown is residential, but on the other side of the Island. As the Trade Center was completed, a large apartment complex was built along the Hudson River nearby. Watching planes crash into the buildings, I had a sinking feeling, a dreadful certainty that this would validate Bush's administration, unleashing his War Lord advisors.

Your cannabis-inspired argument about science vs. religion is garbled, illogical, and full of obviously false assertions. For example: "We are so steeped in vulgar belief that science holds all answers to all problems that no one even doubts it or questions it. It suffers the same problems as religion. Namely, if science is so all knowing why is it the chief source of modern fuck-ups?" No scientist I have ever known claims that science has "all answers to all problems." In fact, university training emphasizes how much scientists in each field of research do not know, and how much past scientific knowledge has been disproved or modified by subsequent work. No educated person thinks that scientists are "all-knowing." You are condemning the ignorance of people who have an uninformed conception of science. That is OK, but to go from the vulgar belief to asserting that genuine scientific knowledge is the main "source of modern fuck-ups" is to assert something that is obviously false. Your examples, DDT and Chernobyl, are examples of the lack of scientific knowledge of ecology and safety engineering—the use of technology with inadequate scientific knowledge. One of the reasons this happens is that new technology is used by people who are not scientists. They are industrialists, politicians, military brass, and so on.

Of course, you are right in asserting that accomplished scientists may lack wisdom and understanding, but surely having scientific knowledge can be an advantage in acquiring wisdom. You would not want to assert that a wise doctor could be ignorant of medical science, or wise anthropologist ignorant about human evolution. You falsely assert that "science can and will rob all mystery from the world." It would be truer to assert the opposite—that advances in scientific knowledge of the past few centuries reveal the mysteries of the world that could not have been imagined in earlier times.

> Zelda is going to the post office, so I'll quit here.
> Charles

October 9, 2001

Dear Charles,

I was glad to hear from you. I was beginning to worry about you. I can't imagine how you are ever in a good mood since your foot has been such a problem for so many years.

I'm not at all surprised that my arguments of the last letter were "garbled, illogical, and full of obviously false assertions." I was so high when I typed it that I'm surprised I said anything intelligible. I use the term "vulgar" to mean common. I have a copy of the Vulgate Bible that I cherish dearly in that it was invaluable to me when I learned Latin. The problem for me is that I learned both Latin and Greek, and I use the words we derive from those languages in the way they meant them.

You say that no scientist you have ever known makes a claim that scientists have all the answers to all problems. I don't say they do assert such a thing. But many of them think that they will eventually know everything, and that some sort of magical age of prophecy fulfilled will ensue. Edward O. Wilson in *Consilience* makes a claim along these lines. He says that humanity must find its way to transcendent existence solely by its own intelligence and will, and that "science is simply the best instrument at our disposal."

You say that I am wrong to assert that genuine scientific knowledge is the main source of modern fuck-ups. You argue that science isn't bad; the people who misuse it are bad. That is the National Rifle Association argument, "Guns don't kill people; people kill people." A gun, like a bit of scientific knowledge, is innocuous and useful until it lands in the hands of an idiot. You can't have science in a vacuum and blame only those who misuse "genuine science." If one is a true scientist he should have enough sense to see that some idiot is going to misuse the knowledge he invents. Worse, he'll tell idiots how to misuse it.

No, I would not want to be treated by an ignorant medical doctor. A computer may have greater medical knowledge than a doctor, and yet it won't have wisdom and understanding. A doctor is at least susceptible of attaining these qualities, and some species of knowledge might help him along. I doubt that the pure scientific understanding of medicine will confer those qualities on him or her.

Science seems far too self-congratulatory and arrogant to me. Are scientists today motivated by pure love of science? Or are they motivated by personal gain, fame, riches, etc.? If fame and riches are primary concerns, and I haven't seen too many scientific discoveries by "Anonymous," then is one more or less likely to open an ill-fated Pandora's Box that could lead to profound devastation in the wrong hands?

I was really glad to hear from you again. I hope this letter is a little more rational. I shouldn't write when I'm high, but that's when I'm most garrulous. I hope the stress of moving passes, and may your dwelling become a home and a refuge. Peace be with you and on you.

Yours truly,
DW

October 18, 2001

Dear DW,

I got an e-mail today from a friend that is right down your alley. Here it is for your amusement:

The date of the attack: 9/11: $9 + 1 + 1 = 11$
September 11th is the 254th day of the year: $2 + 5 + 4 = 11$
After September 11th there are 111 days left to the end of the year.
119 is the area code to Iraq/Iran: $1 + 1 + 9 = 11$
Twin Towers—standing side by side, look like the number 11.
The first plane to hit the towers was Flight 11
I have more:
State of New York—the 11th state added to the Union
New York City—11 letters
Afghanistan—11 letters
The Pentagon—11 letters
Ramzi Yousef—11 letters (convicted for orchestrating the 1993 WTC attack)
Flight 11—92 on board: $9 + 2 = 11$
Fights 77—65 on board: $6 + 5 = 11$

Oh my God! How worried should I be? There are 11 letters in the name David Pawson. I am going into hiding NOW. See you in a few weeks. Wait a sec, just realized "YOU CAN'T HIDE" has 11 letters! What am I gonnado? Help me! The terrorists are after ME! I can't believe it! Oh crap, there must be someplace on the planet Earth I could hide! But no: PLANET EARTH has 11 letters, too!

Maybe Nostradamus can help me. But dare I trust him? There are 11 letters in NOSTRADAMUS." I know, the Red Cross can help. No they can't, 11 letters in THE RED CROSS, can't trust them. I would rely on self defense, but SELF DEFENSE has 11 letters in it, too.

Can someone help? Anyone? If so, send me email. No, don't SEND ME EMAIL has 11 letters. Will this never end? I'm going insane! GOING INSANE??? Eleven letters!

Noooooooooo!!!! I guess I'll die alone, even though I'LL DIE ALONE has eleven letters. Oh my, I just realized that America is doomed! Our Independence Day is July 4th—7/4—7 + 4 = 11

Dave

P.S. IT'S BULLSHIT has 11 letters also.

October 23, 2001

Dear Charles,

Thanks for the humorous piece you sent on number 11. Contrary to your belief, however, I have no interest in numerology. However, I do not agree with David's method of criticism. Ridicule is the easiest form of criticism. He invents all sorts of 11-lettered constructs, whereas the supposed case was based on the immutable historical facts of 9/11. To me a better technique would be a statistical survey of all the things on that day which added to other numbers, or all other major events on another day which added to eleven but had a positive effect. Basically showing that what things add to has no bearing whatever on their inherent nature. Numerology is probably worthy of ridicule, but when you ridicule people you only entrench their beliefs. A fool destroys, but a wise man edifies with his speech. So I agree with Dave, but I dislike him. He goes through life with certainty that his mentality is superior to everyone else.

I did study the part of Qabalah called Gematria. It is similar to numerology, but differs in key respects. First, it applies only to words written in the Bible in Hebrew, putatively transmitted directly from

God's mouth to the ears of its scribes. I made a cursory study of it, but it never did anything for me. What I like about Qabalah is its poetic and metaphorical aspects. The naming of things is important. Our deepest thoughts are unconscious. We need metaphors and similes to translate them into something that we can understand. For example, William Hamilton's metaphors of "selfish and spiteful genes" served wonderfully in Richard Dawkin's hands to make evolutionary science comprehensible.

Even though we have been forced into extreme positions owing to our debates, never doubt that I love science and recognize its contributions to humankind. I just see that T. H. Huxley's intention to have science replace religion as the authoritative source of information about life and the cosmos, which has succeeded beyond his expectations, has had negative consequences. It creates an ethical vacuum that isn't being filled.

Just as I have criticized the fuck-ups of unbridled science, I see how goofy-assed religion inspired zealots to destroy the World Trade Center and has led on both sides to war in which many people will die for nothing worthwhile to them.

As always, your friend,
DW

November 29, 2001

Dear Charles,

I've been lazily lying around for the whole week, thinking about getting up and writing some letters. It took until today to convert intention into action. Congratulations on reaching your 78th birthday. That's impressive. I was going to say, "Oh, you're Scorpio. No wonder you don't believe in astrology!" But I am afraid you will think I am serious.

Thanks for the $50. I needed some new guitar strings. There's anxiety in being on your last set of strings, knowing they're subject to break at any time, and not having any on order. I was also able to resupply my cabinet with things like multi-vitamins, aspirin, Vitamin C, shampoo, and soap. It's probably only psychological, but I feel better when I take vitamin supplements every day.

So what do you think of this war in Afghanistan? Even more, what do you think of Bush's threats to jump on Saddam again? I don't doubt that cowboy W would like to finish what his dad left undone. Though I love America, and I'm glad I was born here, I'm probably better off on death row than are many free citizens of other countries. I'm still shocked by the events of 9/11. Nevertheless, we are the most self-deluding, self-congratulatory people on the face of the earth.

I can't believe how much our freedoms have been stripped since 9/11. I can't believe how frightened politicians are, so that they give away our freedoms to "preserve our way of life." If you trade freedom for safety beyond a certain point you are a coward. We have sold out our birthright in our cowardice.

What gives you such faith that science can employ reason to govern social evolution? What science deals with Bin Laden? And, inasmuch as you have exempted science from any blame, but point to "misuse of science," what is the proper or right use of VX nerve gas, or Sarin, or Ricin? Can you free science from paradox? Can there be truth where paradox is possible? The fact that—I was interrupted here for about five minutes, signing out some library books, and I have no idea what I was going to say after "the fact that . . ." I'm sure I had a string of questions. I remember one, though. Would a society based on reason be a prison for people who desire faith over reason? How could you placate them? And would it be reasonable to just kill them? Or punish them until they relented and accepted your ideas?

I can't see how we can ever reconcile humanity's competing beliefs. Especially when believing people assert that they do not merely believe but know. Everyone looks at the world through the particular lens of his nature and experience and declares that "this is the way the world is" and not "this is the way I see the world." To me any positive assertion of knowledge is a conceptual cave from which to safely view existence. Everything humans do suggests it. We establish homes and communities and occupations in order to create "ground" amidst the formless chaos. We establish routines to make orderly our time, whether its reading the newspaper every morning or walking the dog—having a set thing to do at a set time creates a sense of order and purpose. If we do this in all of those things, why do not the same strong tendencies appear in our ways of conceptualizing the universe and human existence? Why wouldn't we create conceptual caves against the uncertainties of existence?

Maybe Doris Day's mom had it right: "Que sera, sera!"

Sorry for the existential angst, but it's me nature, guv'nor.

DW

3
The Year 2002

7

Death Row Will Be Moved

January 24, 2002

Dear DW,

I am glad that we visited during the Christmas holidays. You looked good. We leave on February 3 for a couple of weeks, first to Phoenix to visit our daughter, then to Santa Fe, where friends from New York have retired.

I am angry about the way our government treats men captured in Afghanistan. The president and other officials in Washington say that we are at war, but they refuse to observe international rules that protect prisoners of war.

I am preaching to the choir. Everyone we know agrees with us, yet when we see each other we repeat it as if we had not said it all the day before. Other than sending an extra check to ACLU or Amnesty International there is not much to do. I went to Mississippi in 1964 to teach Freedom School and canvass people to register to vote. Zelda and I attended protests against the war in Vietnam. There is hardly anything like that going now. We are reduced to talking to other elderly, like-minded people, and to our children.

The talking heads on TV last night said that Bush has 83 percent approval by the American public. Not a single person I know approves of Bush, the vice-president, or other administration figures. The majority of the American people voted against Bush. Opinion polls assume that people continuously change their minds about important subjects. This is a false conception of social reality.

Yours,
Charles

January 26, 200

Dear Charles,

I can hardly believe that it's the last weekend of January already.
hurt my back doing dead-lifts on the weight machine, and I've bee
practically bedridden since then. It hurt to sit, or lie down, and n
position was comfortable for long. I'm slowly recovering.

As I said during our visit, but in response to your written commen
now, I agree with you on the John Walker Lindh thing. The choice
he made, first to study Islamic religion, and then to go to Afganistan
he made long before September 11. How could he have foreseen tha
America would wage war on his new people? As far as we know, h
never shot at any Americans. But we have to have vengeance becaus
he chose them instead of us in our righteousness. He didn't do any
thing of note as far as I can see, and he faces more time and hatre
than robbers and rapists, and even some murderers. Still, our view
very much in the minority.

I found out that the state legislature will approve a proposal to sus
pend the state law that says that death row prisoners are to be held i
the care of the warden of the Indiana State Prison. They want to refui
bish death row starting in the first week of July, and will move us t
the Maximum Control Complex in Westville, ten miles south of her
We were there for a month and a half in 1994 following an attempte
mass escape. It sucks. It's a "supermax" prison, designed to be oppre
sive as hell. There is nothing we can do about it. The Legislative Co
rections Committee passed the bill unanimously. We will be goin
without a doubt. We'll probably be gone for about six months.

I look forward to getting Frans de Waal's *Good Natured: The Origi
of Right and Wrong in Humans and Other Animals.* I finished Edwar
O. Wilson's book. I enjoyed thinking about some of the concepts i
it, but, in the end, he thinks there is some sort of scientific formula
governance that will solve mankind's problems. To me, that notion
no different than "the Noontime of the Magicians." Debates abo
science, religion or/and "ism" are unsolvable. Why? Because huma
mindsets come in four flavors: logical, empirical, emotional, and intu
itive. These domains are linked together by four biases as diagramme
below:

A scientific bias arises in one who likes to view the world in tern
of observation and logic. The artistic bias arises in one who views th
world through feeling and intuition. You'd think the opposites woul
argue the most, but it's actually those with adjacent biases who suff

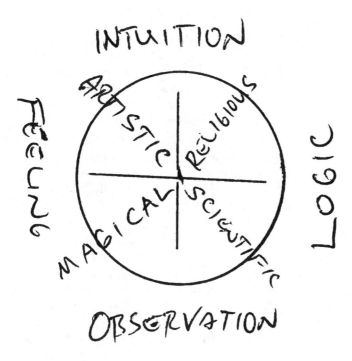

. **Four flavors of human mind-sets.**

he most turmoil. They see the world the same as each other on one
lane, but not at all on the other. A religionist and a scientist will both
epend on logic and esteem it. The religionist believes in the "revela-
ion" of intuition, whereas the scientist can abide only what is observ-
ble or empirical. They both use logic to get to their respective points,
ut neither can understand, or value, the points the other esteems.
Jntil humanity evolves to the point where it can simultaneously work
1 all four spheres or fields, and thus eliminate conceptual biases alto-
ether, it will continue as it has, slowly and painfully. Even as I write
am designing a biochip that, when implanted, will cause anyone who
ngages in biased thinking to flagellate themselves with a barbed flail
or the whole duration of their holding forth on any topic whatsoever!
   I hope all is well with you and Zelda.

                              DW

February 20, 200.

Dear DW,

Here is the book *Good Natured*, by Frans de Waal. I enjoyed reading it, and hope that you will too. In the 1950s, studies of primate behavior in the wild, rather than in zoos and other places of captivity, became a major topic among anthropologists, led by one of my teachers, Sherwood Washburn. He trained a number of young biological anthropologists during that decade and into the '60s. Their work drew large audiences at the anthropology meetings, and I followed it fairly closely, though it wasn't relevant to my own research.

An interesting aspect of this book for me is that the bibliography has no entries for Sherwood Washburn or students of his such as Irven DeVore at Harvard or Phyllis Dollinow at Berkeley. Washburn was one of my teachers at the University of Chicago. He later became a major professor at Berkeley. De Waal has little detailed analysis of the social structures of primate groups. He relies on psychological characterizations of species and individual animals, though his central point is that moral sentiments emerge in organized social contexts. He draws primarily on his own research with animals in captivity. It is difficult to study free-ranging primate groups in their native habitats. Washburn asserted that those living in captive colonies acted very differently from those that were free, that primates caged in zoos were neurotic, and those used for experiments in laboratories were insane compared to members of their species in the wild. De Waal doesn't seem to have done much, if any, ethological research in primate home lands. Even so, I learned a lot from this book.

Yours,
Charles

February 20, 200.

Dear Charles,

I've been recovering from back pain and am working out again, but have to be very conscious of where my back is in every exercise. Getting old is hell, isn't it? Maybe this death sentence stuff isn't so bad after all.

I'm angry about the way our government acts in general, not just with the captured fighters from Afghanistan. They call winter spring, and day night, piss on our heads, and tell us it's raining. Too many people accept what they say without question. September 11 was a terrible thing, but mindless patriotism, the cheerleading media, and Ashcroft, and rattlesnake-eyed George W's threats and posturing leave me with a foul taste in my mouth.

I agree with you about the banality of Christian formulas like suffering is God's Will, and God has a plan for you. If there is a deity who created the universe—and possibly myriad other universes about which we know nothing—taking into account the fact that our little planet is small against the sun, which in turn is a dust mote in the billions of light-year sea of other dust motes, I can't believe it would zone in on this one little planet and arrange personal tutorials for each of its six billion human inhabitants by making "everything happen for a reason."

People die because everything living dies. That is the reason. It is not to teach us strength, or anything else. In all the vastness of the universe, how can any one of the six billion humans—even if he is a "one in a million" person, there are still 6,000 others just like him—thump his chest and pretend he has a significant role in the universe? It's like the fly that sat on the axle-tree of a racing chariot and exclaimed, "My, what a dust I raise!" That the God of the entire universe would choose this little ball of mud for His final revelation is ludicrous.

I was really down when a girlfriend dumped me one time. An acquaintance said cheerfully, "Everything happens for a reason." I was very close to knocking him on his ass. If he asked why, I would've shrugged and explained that "everything happens for a reason!"

I don't think they've decided where they are going to move us yet. If they move us to the Maximum Control Center, it's only 15 miles south of here, so it is not likely to improve the frequency of our visits. Moreover, at that place you have to visit through heavy glass partitions and by telephone. It's a behavioral modification place. It really sucks.

I received my first copy of *The American Poetry Review*. Thanks for this gift; I had never even heard of it. I like poetry and enjoyed the first issue.

Until next time,
DW

Friday, March 15, 2002

Dear DW,

I picked up the enclosed money order yesterday at the post office and want to get it in the mail to you without delay.

We had a good trip to Phoenix and Santa Fe. We decided to return to Santa Fe for a month. Our friends found a splendid two-bedroom rental not far from the center, and with a view overlooking the city We will drive out in a leisurely manner, getting there before the summer opera season ends. Best of all, we will have a sustained visit with creative friends we have known for many years.

I hope that you are moved to a place we can visit more easily. You say that the Maximum Control Center will be worse than where you are now. Since the prison in Michigan City is grim, it is hard to imagine what may be worse. Let us know if you learn when the move will occur.

Is there any progress on your case? During our visit you said that your lawyer was dedicated to work on your case and would find out whether the fingernail evidence of struggle with her killer by the murdered woman has been preserved. You said that at one time you wrote a letter to her sister, Diana Harrington, seeking forgiveness by confessing the murder, but she was unforgiving. You confessed to her in detail, but did your letter include having had an accomplice? What would be gained if DNA shows that another person was also involved in the crime? Has your DNA been tested yet? You were anticipating that it would be when we visited you.

Best,
Charles

April 17, 2002

Dear Charles,

We are in the midst of the annual "cell standardization lockdown, shakedown." We've been locked down since All Fools' Day. Soon they will come and shake us down. They count how many books and pairs of underwear you have. If you have more then the prescribed limit they seize the excess and write you a "conduct report." Then you go to the kangaroo court and receive a sanction. A dramatic pageant dis playing that the Penal God is all-powerful, and that we must bow our heads before His mighty countenance. That's how prison is. Everything is calculated to beat you down. Mostly it works. However many learn to rise above it and see it for what it is. That makes them dangerous when they are eventually let out and on the streets again.

The primate behavior book arrived, but it was seized on the grounds that it came from a private source, and not a publisher, vendor, or accredited college or university. Another ritual of control. I'm going to have it mailed back to you.

Thanks for the money order, I used $25 of it to buy a walkman radio so I'll have some music when they move us to the Maximum Control Center for the renovation of the death row here in Michigan City.

The TV you got me is clear plastic—you can see right into its inner workings. It's the same with the Walkman: its case is clear plastic. It's a sad statement about our society when catering to prisons becomes profitable enough for manufacturers to retool for prison specific products. Sigh.

Peace,
DW

April 24, 2002

Dear Charles,

I'm enclosing an article that demonstrates what happens when scientists over-intellectualize things. You get scientific apologists for pedophilia. Granted, it may not irreparably damage a child. Still, all sexual experiences in early life play into the psycho-sexual development. Abnormal acts bend the psyche. The Rind study has become a stepping stone to further encroachments across the boundary with which we protect children. Its theses became premises for bolder syllogisms. It seems bad to me when science undermines moral, ethical, or common-sense values. What do you think?

Yours,
DW

[Enclosed with letter: clipping of an article by John Leo from *U.S. News & World Report*, April 22, 2002, which refers to a 1998 Rind study published in the *American Psychological Bulletin*. The article says, "The study's conclusion that child sex abuse 'does not cause intense harm on a pervasive basis' was the highest-level endorsement yet of the no-harm rationalization for child sexual abuse."]

May 10, 2002

Dear DW,

I hope the lockdown/shakedown is over by now. You told me about this cruel practice when I visited you some time ago. Prison authorities must sleep well, confident that they are doing a job society wants done and that those they humiliate deserve what they do to them.

The Frans de Waal book on primate moral behavior was returned, with $3.95 postage. What a waste. They opened the Priority Mail envelope I got at the post office, and could see that the only thing in it was a book. Yet they refused to pass it on to you. I have a university mailing label, which would have made the package acceptable. And will use it to mail the book back to you. I will also enclose a book by Noam Chomsky called *9/11*. I know you admire Chomsky. I enclose a clipping from the *New York Times* which says that *9/11* has sold over 115,000 copies, and is on bestseller lists. I bought it for you but read it first. I was disappointed, not by Chomsky's interpretation of events, but by the fact that he did not write it. It is just a collection of re-printed interviews with him. People would anticipate that he is skeptical about the governmental response. Everyone we have talked to in Bloomington, Berkeley, and Seattle, or by phone in other parts of the country, is as critical as Chomsky.

The headline of the clipping from *U.S. News & World Report* asserts that a book by Judith Levine is an "apology for pedophilia." I haven't seen the book, but I am skeptical that this is a fair description of it. Joycelyn Elders, who wrote the foreword to the book was appointed surgeon general by Bill Clinton. His Republican enemies succeeded in forcing Elders' resignation by charging that she advocated masturbation. I would have to look at the Levin book to have an opinion about it. I take issue with your comment on the clipping: "It seems bad to me when science undermines moral, ethical, or common sense values." You ask, "What do you think?" I think that if the implementation of values is done in the light of knowledge gained through sustained and well conducted scientific research (a lot of poorly executed and otherwise inadequate science exists) this must improve the moral order in our society.

The one time I have seen child pornography was years ago in the red-light district of Amsterdam. The pictures were woefully drab and shocking.

When publicity about Catholic priests began to build a few years ago, I thought that the harmful consequences of early sexual experiences may not always be as harmful as the victims, their families, and lawyers claim. They want money, and lots of it. Of course, the claims to suffering may often be true, but were all of these people as traumatized by childhood sexual experiences as they claim? Or, did otherwise dysfunctional families also have a lot to do with it? I ask these questions because I grew up with unhappily married parents, a mother who didn't like me, and a father who didn't care one way or the other. I experienced some sexual abuse by an older brother when I was five or six years old. I barely remember it. Later an older boy introduced me to oral sex and mutual masturbation. Although I suffered sexual confusion and misery, this was as much a consequence of the bigotry widespread in our society, and poor parenting, as it was the result of childhood abuse.

With respect to what Washburn said about the insanity of primates confined in laboratories and zoos, he was talking about the adaptive character of primate behavior. If my memory is correct, he said that when primates are captured, caged, and tested in laboratories, they become neurotic. Mothers fail to care for their babies and often kill them. The divergence of behavior in captivity from behavior observed in field studies provoked Washburn to say that the experimental psychologists studying primates in their labs were observing "insane" animals.

My guess is that people who become criminals already have serious psychological problems. If they are imprisoned for long periods, or if they are put in solitary confinement, I expect their psychological problems will become more pronounced. I also think that conventional behavior in families or larger social groups, and even in whole nations, can become aberrant, or, if you will, insane; for example, notorious and extensively organized activities in Nazi Germany, Pol Pot's Cambodia, or, currently, in Israel/Palestine. I agree with you that the term *insane* means different things, which we understand in the context of its usage. Often we deliberately use words to simultaneously mean different and even incompatible things. Key terms like *sane/insane, nor-*

mal/abnormal, natural/unnatural, rational/irrational, or *evil/virtuous* are loaded with possible meanings.

I look forward to hearing from you.

Charles

May 20, 2002

Dear Charles,

The lockdown and shakedown are finally over! The purpose is diabolical, rather than the mere sadistic impulse you suppose. It is a crafted ritual to maintain control by creating an overwhelming sense of futility in prisoners. Unfortunately, this has consequences that don't really manifest until one is back in the society that wants prisoners to suffer indignation. You have learned that you can take more pain than you thought possible, and another part of you has learned that you're now prepared to dish out more pain than you thought possible. You would not believe the rage that prisons shape and focus. Then they let us out.

You have just witnessed one of the petty cruelties which policy inflicts on every prisoner, the book rule. This is one among hundreds of similar policies you will never see, but with which we live every moment of our lives. People think that "getting tough" is the solution. The fact that recidivism is well over 50 percent indicates that this policy is wrong, but advocates claim it hasn't been pursued with enough zeal. If officials just get tougher, surely we'll break. Ah, but we were broken to begin with. Toughness merely hardens us.

I received the books you sent. I let Obadyah read Chomsky's *9/11* while I started on the monkey book, *Good Natured.* It is very interesting so far.

I enjoyed the piece on brain-imaging and neurotheology I sent you. The subject is fascinating because it shows that "God is in the neurons." I take that to mean that He is a product of the neurons, not as evidence of the reality of God.

I dislike the Rind report in the 1998 *American Psychological Bulletin,* which declared that sexual assaults on children don't seem to harm them. It was a metanalysis of earlier studies that may or may not have indexed the harm caused by pedophilic attacks. The chief pedophile where I am is Chris Stevens, after whose case Indiana founded "Zachary's Law." He is unrepentant and tries continually to justify his predation of children, even his murder of one. If pedophilia were legal, he reasons, the boy's threat to tell on him wouldn't have made him have to kill him. It is all society's fault for not understanding that children are sexual beings who may consent to sex acts. His favorite "scientific proof" is . . . you guessed it, the Rind study, which declared that it wasn't apparent from existing research that any real harm occurred to prepubescent victims of pedophilic assaults.

I agree with you about the Catholic Church scandal. Hell, if I'd known a Catholic priest when I was little, I might try to get a little spending money with a horrid tale.

Until next time,
DW

June 4, 2002

Dear DW,

Childhood trauma and sexuality are central themes in Freudian psychology. I read a lot of Freud and took a course from an analyst, Bruno Bettleheim, at the University of Chicago. He was the director of a boarding school for disturbed children. On one evening every month he met with parents who wanted his advice about their children. His reputation as a scholar led us to accept his authoritarian manner, but no evening passed without his castigation drawing tears from a young mother. We were convinced that sexual trauma caused by seeing parents engaged in sexual intercourse, or a person with an amputated limb, could ruin a child's whole life. Movies, novels, and television spread these and other Freudian ideas throughout American society.

I think that this is a source for accusations in the 1960s and later that nursery school children were violated by their caretakers. Other adults claimed they had "recovered memories" of sexual assaults in childhood. Some people, caught up in publicity about these affairs, confessed to having participated in satanic sexual orgies with children. My skepticism about recovered memory in those events spills over into skepticism about people who come forward twenty or so years later to claim that they suffer from childhood abuse by priests.

The Catholic scandal seems less horrible to me than Guantanamo, or the millions, even billions, of dollars that corporation executives rip from the economy. Today the *Times* has a story about the CEO of the Tyco Corporation who was paid over a hundred million dollars a year and yet cheated on the sales tax for art he purchased in New York by faking a claim that it was mailed out of state.

I enclose a postal money order, and a clipping from the *Times* describing the death row in a new supermax prison in New York state. In effect, prisoners are held in solitary confinement. Is this like the one you will be moved to? It sounds dreadful .

Yours truly,
Charles

June 29, 2002

Dear DW,

I went again to the library to read about your arrest in the January 1980 issues of the *Evansville Courier*. I am again surprised at how quickly the police accumulated evidence against you, and that the prosecutor decided at once on the death penalty. Everything was fast, including the decision to move the trial to another city.

What I read makes me want to talk to your parents and other family members. I try to imagine myself at the age you were then. At that age I was a cadet in the Army Air Corps. At 18, before joining the army, I had taken off for Chicago without consulting my parents, and with only the train ticket and $10 in my pocket. I found a room on skid row for 50 cents a night, and jobs to support myself while I registered for two courses at the night school of the University of Chicago (my Dad, pleased that I was supporting myself, paid the tuition). Thus, I discovered anthropology before going into the army.

Other times, other worlds,
Charles

July 17, 2002

Dear Charles,

Greetings, friend. I've been working on a writing project for friends in Oregon. One of my friends from there is coming for a visit on the 25th and 26th. I've typed 60 pages of single-spaced sheets. I am sick of typing. Sick of writing.

I will write a proper letter soon. Just wanted to let you know that all is well, and that I haven't forgotten you.

May you and Zelda abide in good spirits and good health,

DW

July 26, 2002

Dear DW,

Your note is a mystery. It only says that you are working on some manuscript with someone. Who? What?

You mentioned earlier that you will be moved to another facility while the death row quarters at Michigan City are renovated. Is there any news about that?

I hope this finds you well. On our last visit you were concerned about a lump on your throat. I thought it might be a stopped up saliva gland, but imagine you thought it might be something worse than that.

The gathering of our children and grandchildren in Bloomington for a long weekend seemed to go well. Now we are waiting to leave for Santa Fe in August. I still would like to meet some members of your family. Will you give me their names and addresses? I will not have time before we leave for New Mexico, but might contact them now to arrange a time in October or November.

Bread and Freedom,
Charles

July 29, 2002

Dear Charles,

Greetings, at last! I'm still sort of sick of typing on this old '60s Selectric. It's the best I have, so I have to work with it. I still have another big typing project I have to do for friends.

I agree with you that much of the trauma we attach to sexual events in a child's life may be exaggerated. Kids are far tougher and more resilient than we give them credit for being. I don't think molestation will necessarily ruin a kid for life. In fact, I had a girlfriend while I was in here whose little boy was fondled by a female babysitter (his cousin) who was herself barely pubescent. She reacted hysterically. I told her that she shouldn't view him as "damaged goods" because he was in tune with her more than with any other person. If in word or deed she radiated that kind of negativity towards him he would indeed be ruined, not by the abuse but by her reaction to it. Of course, I became an unfeeling person, and we quickly parted ways.

I enjoyed Noam Chomsky's book more than you did. I agree with him that the U.S. is a terrorist state. It meddles everywhere, breeding powerful resentments. I blame a lot of this on the corporate input into government policy. Oil especially has dictated Middle East policy. I wish our government really was "of, by, and for the people," but it is not. You can't have such a thing owing to the fact that the people are indolent idiots who want someone else to do all the work for them. Unfortunately, the politicians who are willing to do that work are often prostituted, pandering assholes. But I love America. I love its people—pig-headed as they are sometimes—and its vistas. I've visited every state in the Union except Idaho, Alaska, and Hawaii. The thought of bombs going off in the places I've been sickens me. I fear 9/11 was just the beginning.

I'm glad there are people like you who go to anti–death penalty functions and rallies and whatnot, but I have to confess that the subject bores me. I've heard the same things over and over.

Why do you want to talk to my family? I hadn't spoken to my father more than once in the five years preceding that fateful day in January 1980. I left home for good at 17. My sisters were like 12 years old at the time, so they didn't really know me either. My father is not a man with much insight into the human psyche. He can disassemble and reassemble any machine made by man. He understands what we would call trade knowledge, but he can't see any deeper than his own reflection in the mirror, and his insight into others is similarly shallow.

I haven't spoken to my mother in seven years. She refuses to answer any letter I write her. It's all just too much to deal with she says. I think, yeah, try dealing with my end of it. It must be terrible for her. I should probably be trying to console her, her having it so much worse than me, and everything. I doubt they'll talk to you. My mom is phobic about outsiders knowing family matters as shallow as "What's in the bread box?" This traces back to her having been the child of an alcoholic father and, I suspect, a possible incest victim at his hands. This is a guess, but when you live around someone for awhile you hit on their complexes sooner or later. She also has no insight into herself. She tries to control everything to forestall uncomfortable situations. In doing so, she makes it incredibly uncomfortable to be around her. She has flirted with alcoholism most of her life. Her brother was a cocaine addict. One sister was a religious fanatic, and her other sister was a sex addict. She avoids emotional turmoil by just denying it out of existence. If you become emotionally disturbing to her, she'll deny your existence until you fade away.

My father's father was an alcoholic. He committed suicide in '62. My father's mother was a religious fanatic who died of cancer in '67. My stepmother's father died in the Evansville State Hospital, hopelessly insane. She was diagnosed as having "hysterical personality disorder." So there's my childhood milieu. Why would you want to talk to any of these people? I don't want to.

As always,
DW

August 31, 2002

Dear Charles,

I hope this letter finds you and Zelda in good spirits and good health. As usual, nothing really new to report. That's life on death row: every day like the one which preceded it, and I've got 8,231 days in (22 years, 6 months, and some change).

No one knows what is happening with the proposed move to the Maximum Control Center while renovation takes place on death row here in Michigan City. Things are said to be on hold because of the budget crisis. No one knows for how long. We wake up never knowing if today is the day we leave or not. It's unsettling. Seems like our regimen is designed to keep us always off balance.

I wasn't trying to be mysterious when I wrote of my typing project. It was merely a record of certain esoteric practices during a 31-day period called a retirement. Every action and thought is recorded. This is sent to those with experience in these matters, and they comment upon any good or bad trends you might be developing, or question you on any conclusions you put forth. It is sort of like a peer review, secret society style. The "friends in Oregon" are the secret society members whose names are unimportant. These practices have enabled me to live mostly above the plane of emotional reaction to events and circumstances in the exterior world, and to expand my awareness of the contents of my interior world. Since all of these things are entirely subjective, it is fruitless to discuss them with anyone other than those who understand this class of phenomena. Since they develop experientially, and the results are often intended to be quite different than the ends proposed (which weeds out fakers and poseurs), there is no profit in discussing their theoretical merits with anyone who has never performed successfully even the most rudimentary examples of these practices. It would be like discussing the great literature with someone who is illiterate and despises literature. Why go there, unless you enjoy arguing with people who don't know what they are talking about?

My youngest sister came to see me two weeks ago. She's getting married next month and, since she doesn't speak to my father, looked to me for a blessing. I gave it. She is the only one in my family I talk with. Still, it was her first visit in two years. We chat on the phone maybe twice a year. The members of my family are strangers to me. I haven't spoken to them in years. Nor do I want to speak with any of them.

I still haven't finished *Good Natured*, but I've enjoyed it so far. I take most of it as agreeing with my position that we differ from other animals only in our ability to extend thought far into the abstract. It is a wonderful capacity, but I call it a "veneer," because it always (not mostly, or often) fails instantly in times of stress, and we revert to our basic instincts.

The fact that people draw together in the wake of something like 9/11 is not evidence of our great civility, but rather a triggering of our herd complex, like cattle huddling for a storm. Civilization is a loosely related group of oases scattered through the desert of our true natures. We cherish this collection because it offers respite from our lower nature. But we will destroy it rather than do what is reasonable when the right stress hits us. I believe this more today than ever. I not only accept that we are merely a very clever type of chimp, I wish everyone would accept it. Why? Because it's always our ridiculous mindset that we are a species beloved of God, superior to the laws of nature.

Well, how's that for a rant du jour? My rants have been recently criticized for not wandering enough. "A good rant should positively meander," I was told. "Yours wandered," the writer said, "but not enough." If I become good enough at ranting, I may graduate to manifesto writing.

Until next time,
DW

September 28, 2002

Dear DW,

We got back from Santa Fe on the 20th, and the next day our son, Mario, arrived for a long weekend. He had been staying with his brother in Indianapolis while taking a four-day course on how to appraise property that the government wants to take when building roads, pipe lines, or power lines. We celebrated the fact that he has just gotten a divorce. He is buying a house, so we gave him some chairs, rugs, and a table to help furnish it. Our place looks better with less furniture.

I just read your letters mailed in July and August. You ask why I want to meet some of your family. Well, I think that this would help me understand you. After all, I am an anthropologist, and anthropologists study social contexts in trying to understand people. Last winter you mentioned that one sister and her husband visited you during the Christmas holidays by driving from Evansville. And in your August letter you mentioned that your youngest sister came to visit you to ask for your blessing. Thus, you do have some family recognition and respect. You say that your father and mother are alienated, but I would like to experience that for myself by talking to them. I would just like to contact them by mail or phone and ask to see them. I would tell them that I correspond with and occasionally visit you, and would like to meet them. Why? Well, just because I am interested in you. You are an intelligent and tragic person, and a mystery to me.

Well, ultimately, everyone is a mystery to me. I try to understand, and often think that I do understand another person. My wife for 56 years, for example, but then I turn at night and she is sleeping beside me and I think how separate and different we are. I know her better than anyone else in the world, but, in a way, we are strangers. I am not puzzled by her. You puzzle me. Maybe, if I had more pieces to the puzzle I would get a glimpse of the pattern of another life.

You describe a spiritual exercise you have recently engaged in as one in which you closely record what you are thinking and send it to someone (or to some group) for analysis. It is a sort of secret society of people with special training that you say cannot be explained to an outsider. But surely it can be described, or no one could ever join the society. You assume I would not be sympathetic and would try to argue, and you say that argument would be worthless with anyone who has not experienced whatever it is the members of the group experience during meditation.

Well, actually, I do know that mystical experiences cannot be reduced to words, though poetry or dance or music might evoke similar experiences. I have had three mystical experiences at different times in my life. They were major personal events, but I can't put them into words that seem adequate to me. I can't create works of art to convey them. They were unsought, unexpected, and transient. I think they lasted only a few minutes, but I was in a timeless frame of mind. I think of those experiences as divine gifts. I suppose that is why I have little sympathy for people who seek mystical experiences by taking drugs, though in the sixties some of my students claimed to have profound experiences of other domains of reality when they took LSD.

It is not that I am hostile to mystical experiences, but I fear the political consequences of putting the irrational at the center of things. We have far too much irrationality there in any case. I know that good people dedicate themselves to cultivating mystical experiences.

Tell me more about the secret society, or whatever it is you were engaged in. If it helps you get through the days and years in prison, it must be a good thing.

Also, give me the names and addresses of your family. Then let me report back to you what happens when I contact them.

Yours truly,
Charles

October 15, 2002

Dear Charles,

I'm not going to give you the addresses of my family. I am at peace with them now and don't want to stir up that pot. Also, I don't know what my mother's current last name is or where she lives. I haven't heard from her in almost a decade. My father lives in Indiana, but I have no idea where, exactly. Finally, if you knock on someone's door and they answer it, don't try to force your way inside or elbow your way past them because you're merely curious about their house. If they invite you in, excellent. If not, let it be equally excellent. If you demand from people what they are not willing to give, then you have an ill-gotten gain. Who can cherish what he has to rip from another? Some things are merely mysterious. C'est la vie.

I have been playing guitar a lot lately. I'm surprised at how good I've become, and yet how much I keep learning. There never seems to be an end to the nuances of guitar playing. The way you attack a note with a pick or finger, subtle string-bending, vibrato, the several ways of muting notes, legato phrasing, and staccato phrasing—there are countless things to explore. It's the best thing I do; it's the most rewarding thing I do.

Yes, of course the spiritual practices can be explained to outsiders—that's how outsiders gradually become insiders. It's not because it's secret that you can't know, it's because you have no experience that you can't know even if I tried to tell you. Let me make an analogy. Suppose I'd told you that I did a writing project on Latin. Say that I was exhibiting methods of executing perfect passive periphrastic phrases. I can explain that such phrases are generally used to express obligation or necessity. You can pass what judgments on that as your psyche projects. Why would I care, even if you were capable of judging my examples?

When you went to college did you say, "I don't need all the preliminary stuff, just tell me what I need to know for my Ph.D.?"

Even if I gave you a beginner's example you could do nothing but project your psychic reactions to it because you have not performed it. One might tell a lazy or undisciplined student to learn the Muslim prayer in Arabic and to observe it all five times every day, and record all his observations about the practice. In that case we would not be in the least concerned with the question of whether there existed a deity named Allah and if such a deity could be contacted through prayer. I can tell you this: there are many things that happen if you perform the five daily prayers without fail for three months. One learns things about one's will, one's laziness, one's excuse-making capacity, one's inward ideas, one's concern for the opinions of others (in as much as one must flop down his prayer rug and pray at prayer time, wherever he may be), and many other subtle things.

By the record he makes we can tell if he really performed the exercise or not. Although no two records will be the same, a few dozen other salient aspects are universal. You have nothing but speculation, theory, extrapolation, and projections of your own beliefs—what you want to be true and what you fear may be true—by which to pass a judgment on anyone's performance of such an exercise. You might convince yourself that you know all there is worth knowing about it without having to actually experience it and produce a record of your experience to your peers. But you can't know. So how could your judgments move me one way or another? It would be like me having an opinion on whether or not good fieldwork was necessary in anthropology based on what I think in the light of what I can't possibly know, when you do know by direct experience. What would you care for my ignorant thoughts on the matter?

You mentioned the lotus position. My chosen asana is called The Dragon, and it is merely to sit on the heels, kneeling. This is one of the first exercises I was given in 1984. It took me seven months to be able to sit like that for one hour with a cup of water balanced on my head without pain, numbness, or any ill-effects. There were countless things I had to overcome in order to do this, and they all happen to one degree or another to everyone who perfects any of the dozen or so prescribed *asanas* (which is Hindu for posture, more or less). My record of the practice was well over two hundred pages. I cannot tell you what agony it creates to master this position. I cannot tell you how much will it takes to bear the pain, numbness, cramps, and so forth. Your first sign of progress is that it would hurt more to get out of the position than to stay in it for a while longer. Then one day you find that there is no position as comfortable as your asana. You learn to still the restless body.

This is not a tenth as tedious as what comes next: Pratyahra and Dharma: stilling the restless mind. These matters are still in the tyro stage. I can't tell you because you do them, not say them. When you do them, certain results occur. If they do not occur, you did not do them, or you did them half-heartedly, or gave up as soon as it became difficult. Most people of the latter category vehemently deny that any good result was there to be had in the first place. A few who fail because of their laziness or weak wills will not say they failed owing to laziness or weak will, but they blame the practice. If they didn't have a result, there was no result to be had.

Anyway, that's mostly what it is about—a psychological odyssey in which you find out that there is no one else to blame for your problems, that you are your biggest problem, and that every gap in your knowledge, of which there are myriads more than you can scarcely bear to admit, is filled in with projections manufactured by your nature and nurture. If you can somehow stop projecting, you will do your fellow humans a great service by being one less source of trouble in the world.

Well, there's more than that, but first, of course, you have to know the secret handshake.

I'm learning Arabic. Just for fun. It has a beautiful script. I have a gift for languages, and the more I learn the easier the next one becomes, probably because there are universals in every language, and once you know what they are it's easier to get a grip on how a particular language relates to that universal function.

> So, until next time, take care,
> DW

December 2, 2002

Dear Charles,

I haven't heard from you in awhile, so I hope everything is all right.

Things haven't been so good here. On October 27 we had a guy killed during afternoon recreation. We've been on lockdown, 24 hours a day in the cell, ever since. Also, since then, they've been harassing us with nightly shakedowns of our cells. It quickly makes everyone grow sullen and agitated. One guy flipped out completely and started talking to himself and imagining that many of us had said and done things to him. He's violent and strong, so if they let him out with all of us whom he thinks have provoked him, he's going to hurt or kill one of us, or one of us is going to have to hurt or kill him.

I have a suspicion that the prison bureaucrats want something to happen so that they can get their previously allocated funds (now frozen because of the state's budget bind) to renovate death row. They'll probably let him out with us when we come off lockdown, and something will probably happen. If you hear of any such thing, raise a holler out there because they knew without doubt beforehand that something very likely would happen.

The District Court denied my habeas corpus petition and revoked my stay of execution. They haven't set a new execution date yet. I'm still entitled to file an appeal with the 7th Circuit U.S. Court of Appeals in Chicago and intend to do that.

Let's see, what else? Oh: my sciatica has been raising hell, shooting lightning bolts down my leg. It is literally a continual pain in the ass.

So, in review, I've been locked in my cell for a month, the state is trying to kill me, my body is falling apart, giving me constant pain. But other than all that, everything is good!

Hope things are well with you and Zelda and the rest of clan Leslie.

Until next time,
DW

December 20, 2002

Dear DW,

The bad news in your December 2 letter made us feel rotten. I wanted to write a long letter, but only managed to get off the Christmas card with a postal money order to prove we think about you.

I imagine the agony of years on death row, lockdown, waiting for news that your habeas corpus petition has been denied, and your stay of execution revoked, but I imagine this in the comfort of a fine apartment, a glass of sherry and salted nuts next to the computer, Handel's *Messiah* on the CD player, and Christmas lights glowing on our balcony.

This old man has no wisdom to comfort you; the world is a mystery to me. After years of pride in the things I thought I knew I realize how ·little I have understood. The Great Truths I think I know are only partially true. One of them is that for many of us this world is hell. Faust, in Christopher Marlowe's *Doctor Faustus* is skeptical that hell exists and asks Mephistopheles where it is located. The answer is:

> Within the bowels of these elements
> Where we are tortured and remain forever.
> Hell hath no limits, nor is circumscribed

In one place, for where we are is hell.
And where hell is there must we ever be;
And to conclude, when all the world dissolves,
And every creature shall be purified,
All places shall be hell that is not heaven.

As if life were not hard enough, we punish each other. We must, we say, protect ourselves.

Love,
Charles

4
The Year 2003

8

The Dreaded Supermax Prison

January 3, 2003

Dear Charles,

Hi. Thanks for your letter. I actually imagined "sitting in a fine apartment, a glass of sherry and salted nuts . . . Handel's *Messiah* on the CD player, and Christmas lights glowing on the balcony." That was such a warm and beckoning picture that I savored it for some time.

I've been learning Arabic calligraphy. It is a beautiful script. The letters seem to lend themselves to being stretched and bent into flowing arcs and curves. I'm learning to do things like this:

Both of these show the same thing: *Bismillah ir Rahman Rahin*—"In the name of God, most kind, most merciful." It's a famous line in Islam: every surah in the Quran begins with it. I've seen it rendered in many other artful ways. I thought these show very well how flexible the Arabic alphabet is.

Someday I'm going to get an Arabic-English lexicon and begin to do stuff like you see on the walls and ceilings of the world's great mosques.

It's amazing to me how able I am to thoroughly entertain myself even when locked in a cell for months and years on end. I am never

8. In the Name of God, Most Kind, Most Merciful.

141

"stir crazy." I can always find something interesting to do. It's a good thing, too, considering my irrevocable career choice.

We may be moving to the MCC (Maximum Control Center) soon. No one knows for sure how soon. This is the dreaded supermax. Everything is harder than here. But with our lockdowns these days it's beginning to seem better.

Well, I'm going to cook supper—Ramen Texas Beef Noodle Soup, Sharp Cheese Spread, and canned tuna. Until next time, may you and Zelda have peace and happiness.

DW

January 6, 2003

Dear DW,

A small item in the *NY Times* said a Utah judge vacated the sentence of the longest-serving man on the state's death row because he had been denied access to evidence that another person was involved with him in the murder for which he was convicted. The judge said the evidence would not have changed the verdict, but it might have changed the sentencing. During our visit you told us that DNA evidence from Theresa Gilligan's fingernails would show that someone else was with you during the crime. Theresa's bent back fingernails indicated that she struggled with her assailant. So did her husband, judging by the fact that you smashed his head with a dumbbell before shooting him. It seems obvious that you had to have help tying up the parents and their children. If DNA proves that someone else was there, the police would be obliged to test the DNA of your associates at the time. You said that no one is more dishonorable than a snitch and that you would never identify your accomplice. Without giving the name yourself, would you be a snitch anyway for seeking the DNA test?

I enclose the item about the Utah case, along with another article that will please you, given your opinion of snitches: Attorney-General Ashcroft is demanding the death penalty for a snitch who made a plea bargain for a lesser sentence. Another article also reveals what a bloody SOB Ashcroft is; this one is about his roundup of Muslims after 9/11.

When the war protest ended yesterday in courthouse square, we attended an evening meeting of the Bloomington Town Council. The council passed an antiwar resolution 8-to-0, with one abstention. The *Times* recently had an article on councils doing this throughout the country, including Chicago, Seattle, San Francisco, even Little Rock! Islamic calligraphy is a high art, and your copy of it is beautiful.

Best,
Charles

January 30, 2003

Dear Charles,

Thanks for the recent news clippings and for the bookmark. Is it real papyrus? I learned hieroglyphs years ago, even had E. A. Wallace Budge's massive dictionary. It was fun to learn, but Egyptian is a pretty crude language compared to the modern Semitic languages like Hebrew and Arabic.

They are letting us out for recreation one at a time for one hour every other day. It's ridiculous. They took every piece of exercise equipment out, so all we can do is walk up and down an empty tier, or take a shower.

We all watched Gov. George Ryan's speech when he commuted all the Illinois death sentences. Since Chicago is nearby, we get all the stations, so it was on here, live, from start to finish. We cheered and celebrated. It won't save our lives, but we loved it anyway. He showed courage and humanity.

Looks like Bush is determined to conquer Iraq's oil. As far as threats to America, Saddam Hussein is way down the line. Since America has decided to be a permanently intervening military power, a small war is necessary every few years just to train the officers and test their mettle under actual battle conditions. You can't keep a top-notch army without a core of battle-trained and tested officers. Plus, we're oil junkies. We'll rob our own mothers for an oil fix.

Well, supper time.
DW

February 11, 2003

Dear Charles,

Greetings from the belly of the beast! They finally moved us, and it sucks! No guitar. No art supplies. Not much of anything you can have on death row in Michigan City. No hardback books are allowed. I lost my *Webster's Dictionary*, my *Greek-English Lexicon*, *Latin-English Dictionary*, Godwin's *Greek Grammar*, and my brand-new Arabic grammar. They took all the books of other sorts that I use regularly, like *777 & Other Qabalistic Writings of Aleister Crowley*, Godwin's *Qabbalistic Encyclopedia*, and several others. It's a bummer. Books are your best and only friends in a supermax prison cell.

The commissary list here is very limited. Still, it's the only game in town.

I just wanted to write some quick change of address notices. For the next year or so you can reach me at

> Donald Wallace #7114
> Maximum Control Facility
> P.O. Box 557 (A5–105)
> Westville, IN 46391–0557

I got your recent money order, and will write a better letter soon. Tell Zelda hi for me.

Your friend,
DW

February 17, 2003

Dear DW,

When can we visit you in Westville? What will happen to your guitar, art supplies, and books? Will they be held for you and returned when you move back to Michigan City? Is there no appeal? Could I write to someone on your behalf? Will your lawyer help get them back?

We fly to Boston tomorrow. Our son's divorce was finalized, and his daughter will be with him during her school break. She is 9 years old and our only granddaughter.

Do you think the large war protests all around the world will have any significant influence in Washington? At least, the bloody politicians will know they do not have the support they claim to have.

I shouldn't dwell on this. At least, we can keep a little sanity by our futile gestures of protest, a privilege, I suppose, of being a citizen in a democratic country.

I also want to protest on your behalf to get your books returned. Any suggestions?

Your friend,
Charles

February 17, 2003

Dear Charles,

Hi. I am still trying to adjust to the new austere regimen. This place is worse than death row was at the Indiana State Prison in Michigan City. The main differences come from the fact that ISP is generally a level 4 prison with two level 5 units in it (Death Row and D-East, the so-called predator unit). It was easy to let us have some level 4 comforts since they existed in the general population.

The Maximum Control Center (MCC) is a level 5 and 6 unit designed for behavior modification and control, a supermax. Even when they think they're going as light on us as they can, it's worse than death row was at ISP. For example, one behavior modification principle is bed-making. We are in cells that are completely closed in. The only way you can see into them is to go to the door of each cell to look through a 5 by 5 inch window. You have to have your bed made to a certain standard by 8 am, or they will come in and snatch all your bedding for that day. This may be reasonable to do with out of control prisoners, but it seems pointless for condemned men. Many more devices are built into the system here.

One more example: you have to be handcuffed behind your back to come out of the cell. But you can't walk forward out of the cell. You must shuffle out backwards. The list of such things is long. Here are some contrasts between ISP and MCC:

Indiana State Prison Death Row	Maximum Control Center
1. Musical instruments such as my guitar, amp and effects pedal	Inconceivable!
2. Cassette recorder/player and three dozen tapes	Inconceivable!

3. Hot pots, cookable foods in full commissary list	Restricted level 5 commissary
4. Satellite TV, 55 channels, including Discovery, History, Learning Channel, and many more, with 5 Video movies a week	7 local stations of which 2 come in badly
5. Keep your own cosmetics, shampoo, razors, lotion, and fingernail clippers	Cosmetics etc. locked in a box outside your cell, dispensed only at shower time
6. Contact visits, 3 to 6 hours	Non-contact visits, 2 hours and you have to wear shackles at all times
7. Group recreation, 3 hours a day	Recreation 1 person at a time for 1 hour a day
8. No time limit on phone calls	30 minute phone calls

I could go on, but you get the idea. Death row was designed to hold and pacify men awaiting execution, MCC was designed to control and modify the behavior of unruly prisoners. They punish us constantly since the very routines of this facility are designed to be punishing. All of our property was taken without due process—$400 worth of musical equipment from me. No one will raise a holler because we're worthless animals who deserve to suffer. The public applauds. The ACLU shrugs and tells us there's nothing they can do.

They say we'll be here for 1 or 2 years. I don't have 1 or 2 years left. So they've taken my musical equipment and other property forever. Why? Because they want renovations for a high-tech death row at Indiana State Prison. Back in the mid 90s the Department of Corrections tried to get a brand new one built in Sullivan County, at the Wabash Valley Correctional Center. That was nixed by political moves. But the department is persistent. They decided if they couldn't get a new death row, they wanted to renovate the old one. But how to get an appropriation for it? I swear I'm telling you truly—they staged a demonstration of how we could open our own cell doors. A lieutenant said he saw some prisoners out on the range at night on the camera monitors, but for some reason this wasn't recorded on tape, like all other shots. The next day an official locked himself in a cell and started jerking on the door while a cameraman recorded him. Miraculously, the door sprang open. What the camera didn't show was the same lieutenant who had observed prisoners out of their cells was punching the button to open that door. They started chaining our doors shut with padlocks. They went to the legislature saying that the cells were so old and rickety we could get out, and showed them the hoax video they made.

I'm enclosing visiting information, but it is more like torture than pleasure to have a visit here. If you don't believe me, try sitting for two hours in handcuffs and shackles.

Until next time,
DW

February 23, 2003

Dear Charles,

On Wednesday they said, "Okay, we'll give some hardback books to you: dictionaries, law books, and Bibles." All other hardback books remain a threat to security I presume. So on Thursday I was out on a visit seeing a new attorney when the property guy brought my *Webster's Dictionary*. He asked the guy out for rec where I was and he told him I was on an attorney visit. So the property guy leaves. Next day I see the lady who's in charge of the property room. I ask her where's the dictionary the guy brought for me yesterday? She didn't know. That night I'm out for rec, and from way across the pod, through several windows, Scott Johnson signs to me that they gave him my dictionary. So I'm still trying to get it. This makes me fear for all my other books. When we moved we were told we could take hardback books. I brought my best and most expensive ones. If they've lost these or given them away to other prisoners, I'll be devastated.

I've been locked up for 23 years and one month. I'm tired. I'm thinking about waiving my appeals. I need peace from this eternal torment. I'm very tired.

I've noticed my morale has deteriorated since I hurt my back and can't meditate. One can, I'm told, meditate in a recumbent position, but I fall asleep. I can't meditate properly, can't have my books, and I'm tired of being fucked with all the time when I bother no one.

They've also relented on keeping us handcuffed while visiting. We only have to wear leg-irons. It's "phone booth" visiting through glass and you talk over a phone. Two people can visit at once, but there's only one phone.

I would like to have E. W. Lane's *Arabic-English Lexicon* if they make one in paperback. I like novels, but after you read them you are finished. Lexicons keep on giving. I wish I could have the ones I brought. I have another friend working on finding me a good Arabic grammar.

Have you ever listened to Handel's *Suite Ario Dante?* It's on the radio as I write this. I have the Walkman and headset I bought in anticipation of coming here several months ago. I like Handel.

Well, I'm going to restlessly pace for awhile now. I have a lot to think about.

Until next time, I am your friend,
DW

February 27, 2003

Dear DW,

Your February 11 letter with the Westville prison address arrived just before we left for Boston. Since they confiscated your hardback books I bought a paperback edition of Gandhi's autobiography. You should have gotten it by now. If the Gandhi book gets through, I can look for other paperbacks.

The day before we left, there was a snowstorm that closed airports from Washington to New York, and the front was moving toward Boston. We went to the airport expecting that our flight would be canceled, but it left on time, and the trip went very well. We got back in time to participate in the weekly Bloomington war protest. Your letter was here explaining the routines of the Maximum Control Facility and today a second letter with more description.

I will write more frequently now that you are in such an awful prison. You have survived so far, who knows what will happen? Maybe the shits in Washington will start their war, and enlist death row prisoners to fight in Iraq. Friends who participated in an enormous antiwar demonstration in Paris sent us pictures of the American contingent. One young man had a sign that read, "Up your Colon Powell."

Peace,
Charles

February 27, 2003

Dear Charles,

Good news! I got all but two of my hardback books. I got my *Greek-English Lexicon* and *Latin-English Dictionary*, too! I can't say why I'm enthralled with lexicons and dictionaries and grammars, but they are my favorites. So, my spirits are considerably lifted now.

Also, I received the Gandhi autobiography yesterday, for which, thanks. I meant to only scan through the front for now and read it later. But it was so interesting that I got hooked and haven't put it down since. So thanks.

Just wanted to share the good news. May you and Zelda be well.

Yours,
DW

March 2, 2003

Dear DW,

I am glad that you liked the Gandhi book. At the time I first read it I also read Benjamin Franklin's autobiography and decided to give a course on how people interpret individual lives, their own and those of others. Unfortunately, during the final decades of my career at the University of Delaware I could only teach the same undergraduate courses over and over. I changed the reading assignments, but could not venture outside my professional specialty.

I was surprised to see the enclosed advertisement in the *Times* for "The Kabbalah Centre" in New York. Your interest in medieval Jewish mysticism is apparently becoming fashionable. At least, there is a market for it that supports a center at an expensive address in midtown Manhattan.

Yours,
Charles

March 12, 2003

Dear DW,

It is Wednesday again, so we will be off to the town square for the weekly antiwar protest from 5 to 6 p.m. On Sunday there will be a candlelight vigil against war in Iraq coordinated with vigils around the world, starting in New Zealand, Australia, Japan, South Asia, the Near East, through Europe to our East Coast, and then across the country, time zone to time zone at 7 p.m.

Will the profiteers of the military/industrial complex and their hired politicians in Washington shake in their boots at yet another massive peace demonstration? They were unmoved by the huge demonstrations in mid-February. Can they ignore one coordinated in cities from Sydney to Kyoto, Mumbai, Paris, and New York, and in smaller places around the world like Bloomington, Indiana?

Keep us posted on your situation.

Zelda and I send you good wishes. This is no help at all, but we send them anyway.

Charles

9

Religion as Mystic Experience

March 16, 2003

Dear Charles

My new attorney did not, and would not, help get my books back. I simply sent an itemized bill for them which totaled $635. It worked. Anything worth more than $300 is considered "grievous loss" by the courts, not to be taken without due process. In any case, no court-appointed criminal attorneys will help us with that kind of thing. For one, you're lucky enough if they aren't too overburdened to handle your criminal case. Second, they are discouraged from meddling with government agencies. If something egregious happens, you might be able to talk one into making an inquiry by telephone or letter.

I have no interest whatever in New Age Qabalah. New Agey Jewish rabbis spell Qabalah with a K to distinguish it from Anglo Saxon occultists. I don't know why they use two Bs. The H as a suffix indicates holiness. Thus, Sara and Abram became Sarah and Abraham when sanctified by God. H is the letter of breath and signifies inspiration of the Holy Spirit. Often you will find the final "h" left off when people are speaking of something like gematria, which is similar to numerology. There is only one value in this sort of numerology. The mind is linear. It moves generally from A to B, but the random generation of numbers that have ideas associated with them jumps you, willy nilly, all across the whole fields of thought. Then a sudden association triggers a line of reasoning that you would otherwise never have got to.

Peace, my friend, and hello to Zelda.

DW

March 28, 2003

Dear Charles,

My concern is "Practical Qabalah," which can't be learned from books. Who thought out the symbols that are the object of meditation of the Qabalist? All the rabbis agree: they were angels!

This seems silly at first. But what are angels, spirit intelligences and so forth that appear in the mystical traditions of every religion? Who are these Divine Beings? Are they merely props in great frauds? Or do they have some basis in fact? Occultists think these beings are the latent capacities of our own higher selves. Devotional mystics don't care. The practical Qabalists arrive at conclusions that can only be understood when you have a clear line marking the subjective from the objective. Easy to say, not so easy to do.

Symbols used as objects of meditation concentrate the mind and stimulate certain feelings. The Qabalist uses symbols to guide thought out into the unseen and incomprehensible. The art of it comes only after years of practice. The trained mind, tracking from symbol to symbol, manages to think about the unthinkable at first through a glass darkly, but practice sharpens the inner eye until the images become luminous. At my still partially developed level, I have talked to angels. Critical reasoning will not take you there.

Does this clarify my position?

DW

April 7, 2003

Dear DW,

I just spent an hour looking for your last two letters. I had tucked them into a recent copy of a journal. At my age this sort of thing happens frequently. Another example: I woke up this morning with two vivid memories and a frustrating effort to recall the word for maggots. The first memory was of an incident one summer in Delaware. I had taken the kitchen garbage out to empty it in a large can in the garage. When I removed the lid I saw a wriggling white mass of maggots. They were repulsive, and in fury I began killing them.

The second memory was of a scene in E.M. Foster's novel *Passage to India*. An elderly English woman who had recently arrived in India was unpacking in her room in the cantonment when she was surprised to see a wasp on a wall peg for clothing. In that moment she was overtaken by admiration for the beauty of another form of life. This was what I failed to do on seeing the maggots. My sense of failure was compounded by inability to recall the word for maggots.

Enough about age: on to the religion by which you "sail to the stars and goose angels out of your path." Your use of symbols to think the unthinkable makes truth claims impossible to refute. Frankly such experiences seem delusional to me. I try to understand the aesthetics of it. What is attractive about thinking the unthinkable, pondering the imponderable, knowing the unknowable? The appeal has to be poetic. This raises the problem of how one learns to distinguish good from bad poetry, shit from butter? You will probably reply that the distinction is knowable only through the ritual practice: the experience of ultimate reality is direct and incommunicable.

Oh my, a little religion talk goes a long way.

I went to an Indiana web site yesterday and read a summary of events over the past year relative to death row (they list some national events, too). It said that Jerry Thompson was murdered on October 27, 2002, but did not tell anything about how it happened other than that he was stabbed. Did you know him?

Yours truly,
Charles

April 11, 2003

Dear Charles,

Greetings! Don't feel bad about the memory losses. I'm just as bad, and I'm only 45. If I live to be your age I'll probably forget my name.

Yes, I knew Jerry Thompson, who you read about on the web. He was a thug, a bully who spread ugliness all around him. I'm glad he's dead.

I would like anything on the Arabic language. I've been trying to get a grammar, a lexicon, and calligraphy examples for months. No luck. I love learning new languages, and they get easier as you go. Having learned four languages so far I've gained insights into human thought and into people who speak each language.

Many people have had some sort of mystical experience. One such experience put me on this path. Before that I didn't believe in such things and had contempt for anyone who claimed that higher states of consciousness existed. Accidental ecstasy while often profound is usually transitory and uncontrolled. Compare a wet dream, when an orgasm isn't fully savored because we aren't conscious, to a well-built Tantric orgasm. Orgasm is a form of Samadhi in that to lose the sense of self is to be "with God." Practical Qabalah is the art of developing ecstatic trance into long-sustained, controlled, and frequent experiences. If you ever have one of the little accidental transcendent moments, which are feeble on this scale, but profound as hell to the first-timer, then you will have your answer of "Why?" The glory of such a short and unfocused event is nothing compared to a long and focused episode.

Is it "delusional," as you suspect? Who cares? Your objections could be judiciously filed under the rubric, *Damnant quod non intelligent*— "They condemn what they do not understand."

Finally, you use the language of logic in a field where it doesn't apply. You can't criticize inductive arts in terms of deductive sciences; or criticize music in terms of mathematics. See Wittgenstein's "Language Game Theory."

> Peace, brother,
> DW

April 24, 2003

Dear DW,

At Borders I ordered paperback editions of books you want: an Arabic grammar and two books on calligraphy. It was so easy I am ashamed that I didn't do this sooner. The clerk said that it would take about ten days to get them.

I had not thought of an orgasm as a form of Samadhi. What you wrote recalled for me the description of orgasm as "a little death." I don't know where that comes from. When I first heard the expression I thought it was a literary trope where you say the opposite of what you mean, like saying "That's BAD" when you mean that's good. "A little death" is a poetic way of saying that an orgasm is a moment of intense life. Another meaning would be that an organism, by possibly initiating a new life, entails death. Another concurrent meaning would be the one you suggest, that the loss of self at the moment of orgasm is a little death.

I enjoyed your letter, but when you refuted something I wrote—that the experience of ultimate reality is direct and incommunicable—you misunderstood my attitude. I was not arguing with you, as I did over the nature/nurture controversy, but was engaged in a dialogue with myself about the systematic cultivation of mystical experiences. When I wrote that this seems delusional to me I did not mean that it is always bad, only that this raises the question of how one will distinguish good from bad potentials in experiences that suspend reason.

I once read a Wittgenstein biography. Friends who were Wittgenstein experts, and the biography, explained his concept of language games, but I have forgotten exactly what it means. Even so, I don't think he thought that language games could be avoided.

I hope this finds you well. I am pleased that it was easy to locate the calligraphy and grammar books.

With good wishes,
Charles

April 28, 2003

Dear Charles,

I got your letter today. Thanks for ordering the books for me.

As for the term "delusion." So we are all delusional most of the time. You are a lover of reason and rationality. I'll join you in admiring them as wonderfully useful tools, but they do not encompass all reality. As for Wittgenstein, I think he was absolutely decrying the use of one domain to criticize or verify another. You can describe religious statements in rational language, but not evaluate them.

Delusion connotes a "misleading" of the mind. But if one learns to generate visions, and to control them, one may then apply them effectively. It is difficult to become wise in their use. The most common pitfall is to objectify one's subjectivity, to start believing angels, demons, gods, or whatever actually exists outside one's own organism.

I can't wait to see the calligraphy and grammar books! There's not much to look forward to in this place. Interesting books are always a joy!

DW

May 3, 2003

Dear DW,

I was disappointed in the calligraphy booklet. It did not have any elegant examples for you to practice. The other one has not come yet, but has the title *The Art of Arabic Calligraphy*, so it may be better. If the grammar I ordered does not seem adequate I will look for another one.

The local paper today has an article about the execution of Kevin Hough on May 2. The last paragraph says that Joseph Trueblood is scheduled for execution on June 13. I hope that they are not friends of yours. Even if they are not, the grim fact is that our government continues in this bloody path out of sight, and cleaned up with medical technology.

Your friend,
Charles

May 15, 2003

Dear Charles,

I got *Arabic Calligraphy: Nask Script For Beginners* and the *Arabic Grammar*, for which many thanks. The calligraphy book isn't bad. It shows the proper strokes for each letter. To tell the truth though, this is an adjunct type of grammar, full of paradigms and nuances, but assumes you already know the basic rules and models of Arabic. I have one like this for Greek, and it's an excellent supplement to my Godwin's *Greek Grammar*. In any case, I can use it, but it will become more valuable when I get the basic grammar.

New Rules: We can receive hardback books of any kind now. Also, they're supposedly checking with Indiana State Prison to see how and what we could order for art supplies there, so that we can order some here. It would be good news if it weren't for the fact that I already have great art supplies there. They took me twenty years to accumulate. Some of them, like calligraphy pens, we weren't even allowed to order any longer, but could keep them if we already had them. Plus, I'm not among the landed gentry, and even quality pencils cost more than $1.00 each. So I'm happy that they may let us get art supplies, but unhappy that I can't have the ones I already own.

I'm so weary, especially now that we've been sent here and had all our property taken. More and more I ask, "What is the point?" I'm in the last stages of my appeals. I'm going to die soon anyway. Why spend the last year in misery? More and more I fail to find reasons to live. Death is peaceful, at least. You're not constantly under attack in the tomb. I contribute nothing to society. I eat, sleep, shit, breathe, and take up space in a concrete box all day, forever. There is no light at the end of the tunnel. There is only one escape.

Yes, I was friendly with Kevin Hough and with Joe Trueblood. In the end, though, we're all men whose lives took terribly wrong turns, irrevocable turns. We live with what we did till we participate in the ritual of our own executions. The world is no better off after that. I hope Joe gets a break because he doesn't want to die.

Sorry to be so depressing, but I'm not going to lie and swear I'm okay when I'm not. Thank God I've broken the bonds of that sort of behavior.

Until next time,
DW

May 15, 2003

Dear DW,

Our daughter is a public health veterinarian specializing in the epidemiology of zoonotic diseases. She took a new job in Washington State and moved to Seattle last November. In January she was in an antiwar demonstration. It was raining and the guy next to her suggested they stop at a coffee shop. A date later it was love and he soon moved in with her. The house she had just bought needs repairs, and he has a lot of carpenter equipment, so they have been nest building ever since. From June 5 to 16 we are going to visit them and learn what this new family member is like.

If there is a long line at the post office, I will not wait to buy a money order, but just mail this letter and get it next week.

We think about you often and hope that you keep your spirits up. I know this is difficult, but you manage much better than I could.

Charles

May 19, 2003

Dear Charles,

I just want to let you know that I received your letter. The outside of the envelope was stamped here "money order enclosed." Thanks. The money is timely. My headphones broke, contributing to the depression I recited in my last letter. They removed the speakers from our TVs, so I had no audio. I have closed-caption, but it takes away from watching TV. I just filled out an order form for a new set of headphones, and this bit of prospective relief from that problem makes life seem more livable. You said I do better than you would in keeping up my spirits, but it's a day-to-day thing.

I hope you have a good time in Seattle. I loved that area when I passed through it at age 14. On Highway 1, just north of Oregon, night found me hitchhiking through primal rainforest. The traffic thinned out to only the occasional car, and all kinds of strange noises were coming from both sides of the highway in the forest. I started thinking about Bigfoot and became filled with fear at each forest noise. Finally, I came to a closed gas station. I clambered up onto its roof and lay down and slept until morning. The forest was beautiful by day.

The program you sent for the Bloomington Early Music Festival sounds like fun. I'm not an opera fan, mostly because I don't understand the words. But I love all kinds of classical music, especially chamber music and violin and piano concertos. Bach's canons and fugues make me almost burst into delighted laughter. They're clever as Shakespearean phrases, which also make me laugh with delight sometimes. Some of his lines from the plays are so exquisitely wrought that they stick forever: "Thou knowest the mask of night is on my face, else would a maiden blush bepaint my cheek for that which thou hast heard me speak tonight." It made me hoot with delight when I read it long ago. I suppose it seems overwrought by today's standards, but its rhythm and rhyme and runes caress my ears. (I suppose by runes I mean its meaning—just got carried away with alliteration.)

Hi Zelda. Your friend,
DW

May 23, 2003

Dear DW,

I looked at the grammar briefly and saw that it did not have lessons for a beginner. I will find a regular beginner's textbook.

It is good to hear that I can send hardback books. The beginning Arabic textbook will probably be a hardback when I find it. Borders now refuses to mail any books to men in prison. This is why I mailed the books with an Indiana University label. It is a stupid rule.

You are right that academics are no more virtuous than other people. Even so, the more we know and have, the more responsible we are to behave virtuously. American academics live very well and are well educated. Thus we should not be as petty and self-centered as we often are. I never recovered from a romantic conception of anthropology as a calling that creates a community of caring acolytes. It is not that now, and perhaps never was, except in my imagination.

Like everyone else, I admire wealth and education when they are well used, but I am most impressed when someone who has limited resources acts in a virtuous manner. I am moved by what you have accomplished, spiritually and intellectually, while locked in a cell on death row. Perhaps this is just a cliché. It seems like ancient wisdom to me.

Peace,
Charles

June 13, 2003

Dear Charles,

Hi. I've been waiting for them to pass out this month's supply of franked envelopes before writing. Thanks for the latest Arabic grammar. It is much better for my needs and has already made the first one more understandable. I always feel best when I'm learning new things, so my mood is lighter these days. Plus having a goal gives you at least one reason to want to stay alive.

I got my new headphones. They cost $30.14 from the commissary. They sound good, but I have a catalog where they cost only $20.75. The state contracted with Keefe Commissary Supply Co. of St. Louis and gave them a monopoly, so we pay outrageous prices for everything.

So now it's big news that Bush et al. exaggerated the case of clear and present danger from Iraq. It was obvious right from the start that the propaganda machine had been turned up full tilt. I could scarcely believe anyone could go for it.

I've been thinking about what you said, that you could say poetry was musical or that music was lyrical and be within the law, so to speak. I suppose you are right. But the fact that you can actually say anything like that shows how language is a trap. The fact that there is no way to understand exactly what you mean by it proves Wittgenstein's Language Game Theory, doesn't it?

What does it really mean to say something to the effect that language is an activity of the mind in which some parts of experience are used to represent others? Wouldn't that mean that some facts are used as symbols to express other facts?

Here's a projection of a three-dimensional cube onto a two-dimensional plane. Notice that it uses 120-degree angles to represent 90-degree angles. Now say, "A right angle of 120 degrees." I agree with Wittgenstein's Language Game Theory because to make moves in one context that only make sense in another context produces absurdities. Although I appear to have drawn them above, there is no such animal as a right angle of 120 degrees. It is not a cube I have drawn, but the illusion of a cube. Our thought, and therefore our language, is rife with such illusions. Therefore, reason has limits, and we can't even know what those limits really are. Reason is but one "dialect" through which experience can be expressed. There are others. I respect reason and logic for what they can do, but I don't give them supreme status.

At least that's my story for today. May you and Zelda be well.

DW

June 20, 2003

Dear Charles,

I wanted to thank you for helping me through a difficult period by sending me several good books. Ultimately the will to live is internal, but others can surely help. I feel ready to settle in and endure this episode in my life.

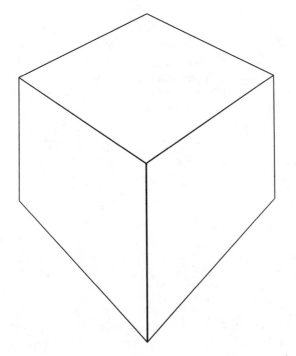

9. Cube.

I'd like to ask one last book favor of you: *The Columbia Encyclopedia*, 6th edition. My friend Mark Wisehart had a 5th edition, and I used it frequently when we were at Indiana State Prison. It cost $75 back then, so I never even fantasized about owning one. Later the sixth edition came out and it cost $125 at first. Again, way out of my league. But now Barnes and Noble has them on sale for $29.95, and they ship to prisons. I don't know how long this sale will last, but I'm willing to forego any books from now on if you would help me get this one.

Wisehart got his sister to order one online from Barnes and Noble. He got it yesterday. He said it has a lot more entries than did his 5th edition, and that especially a lot more hi-tech and computer stuff. Unfortunately, here I can't borrow his. But now, at $30, they're in a range that offers hope. If you can help, please do, and I'll abide with no future books.

DW

June 25, 2003

Dear DW,

I bought a money order yesterday to send you, but was planning to write a letter to go with it. Your letter about *The Columbia Encyclopedia* arrived just now, so I will order it on my way to the post office if they don't have it in stock.

Meanwhile, I should read Wittgenstein before writing, but I never owned or studied any of his books. I gave away an excellent biography that summarized his ideas in the context of his life. I will send you a copy of the entry about him in an *Encyclopedia of Philosophy*, which fortunately I did not give away.

Anyway, I am off to mail this, and to Barnes and Noble.

Charles

July 11, 2003

Dear DW,

You should have the *Columbia Encyclopedia* by now. I was surprised by the size and that it was boxed. Impressive.

When I went to mail the encyclopedia I looked in the philosophy section to see if any books by Robert Fogelin were there. There was one, just published, so I bought it. He is a Yale Ph.D. who lived next door to us in Claremont, California. When we left Pomona College, he went to Yale as a professor and I went to New York University. We visited back and forth, but Bob got fed up with Yale philosophy department bickering and accepted a chair at Dartmouth. I have read several of his books and feel like he is "my philosopher," he and another guy, Mort Beckner, a philosopher of science who was in our poker group at Pomona College.

Fogelin's book is *Walking the Tightrope of Reason: The Precarious Life of a Rational Animal.* It has the virtue of brevity and great clarity of exposition, so I sat down and read it through right away. Earlier you had used Wittgenstein's "language games" in a way that struck me as incorrect.

What seems wrong to me is the "therefore you can't count on reason or logic because they depend on thought/language." In fact, you and I do most of the time count on reason and logic. If we didn't we could not argue with each other. We reason about things, each one assuming that the other one is a rational animal. Of course, our reasoning skills are limited, and we appeal to other sources of knowledge: our experiences of the world, and what other reliable people claim to be their empirical knowledge, aesthetic experiences, and so on. I do not dichotomize reason and empirical knowledge. It seems to me that common sense combines them, that they depend on each other, that emotion, cognition, and reasoning skills are joined in our experiences of the world.

The amazing thing to me is that your letter came right at the time that I discovered Bob Fogelin's book.

Yours,
Charles

July 12, 2003

Dear Charles,

As you can see, they put some pencils on commissary. They're just cheap no. 2 pencils, so one can't work wonders with them. But they're worth hours of fun, anyway. I'm sure glad to have them. There's hardly anything as full of potential as a pencil and a blank piece of paper!

Thanks for the $50. I used $22.25 of it to order books from Edward R. Hamilton. They're sort of a publishers' clearinghouse, and often have excellent books for ridiculously cheap prices. And they send catalogs often. For me it's a chance to order an eclectic mix of titles I would never have dreamed of asking anyone for, partly because I hadn't even heard of any of them!

I've been practicing my Arabic and Arabic calligraphy. The language is coming along well. The calligraphy is hard to do without calligraphy pens, but pencils make it easier because you can lightly sketch something before entering the "do or die" arena of indelible ballpoint ink.

I didn't know the biographical stuff about Wittgenstein. True genius seems almost always eccentric. One is isolated by having a singular view of life. Among a troop of chimps it's a very important daily ritual for the males to run to and fro, screeching, shaking foliage, and swelling up in threat displays. It helps them sort out social order. But imagine one chimp looking on with a human intellect. Even if he could summon the heart to play along, he'd be alone. His desires and values would be on a plane that was his alone. The other chimps would probably kill him, drive him away, or abuse him as an omega male. We're just a brighter type of chimp, and true genius knows it.

I'm only slightly brighter than average and I see the differences between my thinking and average thinking very clearly and often with frustration. But I'm close enough to the rabble to still be able to relate and understand them—to even share their motivations. What if you were witness to such profound insights that you could not help but want above all else to share them with others—to commune in the moment of "do you see?" But no matter where you looked you found that in comparison to you people were no more than average 4th graders.

I guess it's a better world today for true genius in that it's much smaller in offering instant communication around the globe. But it is awful to look at the state of the world and see mankind for the terrible

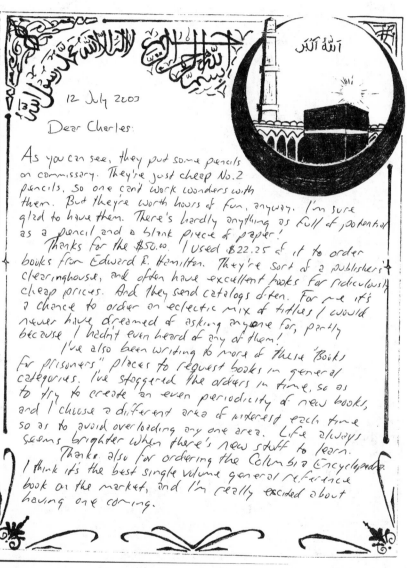

12 July 2003

Dear Charles:

As you can see, they put some pencils on commissary. They're just cheap No. 2 pencils, so one can't work wonders with them. But they're worth hours of fun, anyway. I'm sure glad to have them. There's hardly anything as full of potential as a pencil and a blank piece of paper!

Thanks for the $50.00. I used $22.25 of it to order books from Edward R. Hamilton. They're sort of a publishers' clearinghouse, and often have excellent books for ridiculously cheap prices. And they send catalogs often. For me it's a chance to order an eclectic mix of titles I would never have dreamed of asking anyone for, partly because I hadn't even heard of any of them!

I've also been writing to more of these "Books for prisoners" places to request books in general categories. I've staggered the orders in time, so as to try to create an even periodicity of new books, and I choose a different area of interest each time so as to avoid overloading any one area. Life always seems brighter when there's new stuff to learn.

Thanks also for ordering the Columbia Encyclopedia. I think it's the best single volume general reference book on the market, and I'm really excited about having one coming.

---

10. Page 1 of letter, July 12, 2003.

troops of chimps of which it's made. Our government uses terms such as "shock and awe" and "brinksmanship," which show that we are just as locked into monkey-ass threat displays for dominance as the basest chimp.

So, my friend, we come again to where we began our discussions of human nature. I'm sure neither has changed his central belief, but I've profited from hearing the other side, and hope to continue.

As always,
DW

July 16, 2003

Dear Charles,

Got the encyclopedia this morning. Thank You! I've been in it all day. Came up long enough to write this note. Now, as the hero in an action adventure might say, "Cover me, I'm going back in!"

DW

July 23, 2003

Dear DW,

Good news that the encyclopedia got to you and that you enjoy reading it. Also, that your study of Arabic is proceeding. The decoration on the opening page of your letter must have taken a long time to produce. It is impressive.

I suppose you want to revive our nature/nurture debate. Well, OK. First, whether human nature or culture is a cause or an effect of the other is a which-comes-first-the-chicken-or-the-egg argument. The rest about human nature is an assertion frequently made by the conservative ideologues who consider it a deathblow to "liberalism." Please don't think I am worried about using an ad hominem argument. In this world who we associate with indicates where we stand. Birds of a feather, and all that.

It surprises me that the ideas of reactionary political activists who would have absolutely no sympathy for your personal situation appeal to you. They rail against the "Enlightenment Project," asserting that the changes that liberals advocate have led to totalitarian states, to failed economies, to the bleeding heart treatment of criminals that increases crime, to weakened military power, and so on. They assert that efforts to cultivate a kinder, more considerate, more egalitarian, and rational society can never overcome the beast that lurks in the human breast.

The folks whose conception of human nature you admire reject "utopianism." They urge us to be "realists," and to get on with making money and with locking up or killing our enemies.

You must infer human nature from observations of cultural behavior and artifacts. If you consider what constitutes evidence for your assertions, it is wise to pluralize the terms *culture* and *human nature*. Since cultures have been changing throughout history, so too must the human natures change. If you observe people in an objective manner then you must consider all the evidence, not just behavior that emphasizes selfishness, brutality, and violence. You must observe people working together, falling in love, marrying, having children and taking care of them, decorating their bodies and homes, preparing food and eating together, playing music, writing poems, praying. Observed over a long period, you will record that people do those things almost all the time. You will see that they sometimes badmouth each other, cheat, and steal, but you will rarely see them acting violently. When threatening and violent events occur, they are shocking to the people involved in them. This is a commonly recognized fact.

Another fact: when one talks to people in different countries around the world about what they are thinking and what they are doing, they explain themselves to you. In short, they reason about themselves. That, dear DW, is because we are, above all else, rational animals! Your letter reduces reason to acts of rationalizing selfish human motives. You set aside the fact that people everywhere spend the overwhelming majority of their time in constructive and peaceful social interactions, even in communities governed by those notorious examples of violence: Nazi Germany, Stalinist Russia, Pol Pot's Cambodia.

In your view the only use of reason is to rationalize irrational desires and actions. If you are correct, any appearance of rationality we attempt to achieve is an act of deception. Would that include your own reasoning? Then, why bother? No one could fool anyone else because we would all know that the other person was falsely presenting himself. You must love the conundrum: everything I say is a lie.

A difference between us is that the appeal of reason to me represents an ideal of a reasonable person. This is a more or less thing. Some people are more reasonable than others, meaning that they observe things with greater subtlety and accuracy, have better judgment when issues are contested and evidence is limited, and they understand their limits (they have less hubris than others). We admire people with these virtues.

Unlike you, I rarely think that I am smarter than other people. For years I remembered having been a mediocre student in high school. Then, in middle age I found old report cards in a closet and discovered that my grades were pretty good. Anyway, my Enlightenment ideal is to become a reasonable person.

Besides the encyclopedia article on Wittgenstein, I will send you a copy of Bob Fogelin's *Walking the Tightrope of Reason.*

Yours truly,
Charles

August 8, 2003

Dear Charles,

Thanks for your letter and enclosures. I'm glad you liked the decorative Arabic letterhead. It took a few hours to do, but I wanted to express my appreciation for your help in my studies and to show that your contributions hadn't been wasted.

I consider ad hominem arguments void. They subvert logic. This is ironic because I am the one who always mistrusts reason and logic, calling them whores. I may share one or more premises with political conservatives, but I don't share their conclusions. Proving once again that everyman dances logic into his own bed even when he picks her up at the same bar.

Accept all evidence? I do, mon ami! I look and see that the world is exactly like it is, all of it, from wondrous and noble to craven and foul. In good times I would never have burglarized homes. But when I needed money, things changed. In good times the USA is tolerant and benevolent. After a 9/11 things get full of jingoistic bluster and you find out how tribal we are. I disagree with Bush conservatives who think you're either fucking or getting fucked—and since some fucking is a given, then let them be the fuckers and not the fuckees. This line of reasoning is very human, but I say that human nature balances things out. It's only when meddlers try to enforce ideas that turmoil ensues.

Also, I do not merely think I'm slightly above average intelligence; I know it and have demonstrated it. To pretend not to notice it would be to affect a false humility, which is more arrogant than simply acknowledging a truth. I was trying to contrast my own alienation by being slightly smarter to how it must be for true genius. For example: On December 31, 1999, MTV 2 played Prince's "1999" video 24 hours straight. Average guys were discussing this. One had the bright idea of "Hey, I bet they're going to play it 1999 times!" Others agreed quickly. But I knew that there were only 1440 minutes in a day. The song is about 3 minutes long, so I estimated they could play it 400 to 500 times maximum, but I said nothing. Let them have their fun. This was small alienation for me; imagine how Einstein felt listening to us. That's all I was trying to illustrate.

Since you made a moral issue of it, I think you are lying to yourself to say you never thought you were smarter than others. How can you accuse others of being "wrong headed" without asserting that you are right headed? Let's not get into an Alphonse and Gaston routine of trying to out humble each other in furtherance of our competitive natures (or cultures, if you like!).

I've been waiting all week for the franked envelopes. Wouldn't you know they'd come on Friday?

Until next time, your friend,
DW

August 26, 2003

Dear Charles,

I haven't finished Bob Fogelin's book, but I really like it.

I was just sitting here wishing I could enjoy a nice, refreshing cigarette. When I was out on the streets, smoking was still a God-given right. Hospitals and doctor's offices had ashtrays in them. No public lobby failed to provide ashtrays. Now things are different. I never had any doubt that smoking was detrimental to health. How could it not be? Nowadays though, I think anti-tobacco politics are hysterical. I liked it better when we grilled big greasy slabs of red meat, smoked an after-dinner cigarette, and then went for a Sunday drive in a big gas-guzzling car without seatbelts.

Nowadays kids ride bicycles with helmets on. If you rode up on your bike with a helmet on in my neighborhood, you'd have needed it to help absorb the ass-whipping you were about to get. Everything seems inordinately pussified these days. I mean, give Darwinism half a chance, for Christ's sake.

I never fitted in this world to begin with, but nowadays it is so alien to me that it seems like another world. There weren't any personal computers, or an internet when I was out there; no one had a cell phone. I've never seen a CD except in pictures. We had records. I know you've seen a lot more change in your life than I have—you may remember when chestnut trees were common in America. It's different when you go away for 25 years and only hear about changes. I'd be in culture shock out there.

Peace,
DW

September 1, 2003

Dear DW,

You say you are inclusive but always use your concept of human nature to explain our vices: our aggression, cruelty, selfishness. You assume that this nature cannot be governed, limited, or sublimated, and that efforts to do so are self-deceptive. I argued that to study nature the first rule is to consider all relevant evidence. While you claim to do this, you turn right around and assert that our nature is to dominate one another, to threaten and kill.

If you will in fact pluralize your thought you will consider the existence of multiple human natures and cultures interacting in various situations over time with each other. Since you will always have limited observations from which to infer a human nature, you will need to locate generalizations in particular historical contexts. This is not to say that generalizations about cultures and human natures are impossible, but most of the time they are banal.

> Your elderly utopian common-sense rationalist friend,
> Charles

September 9, 2003

Dear Charles,

Thanks for your letter. You always have some interesting news. I, on the other hand, hardly ever do. Every day here is just like the one preceding it.

Yes, it makes sense to examine who advocates a particular argument. You say it "gives you information about the social and historical context in which the argument occurs." I shorten that to say that who may indicate why. Politicians have an agenda and seek to justify it; that's human nature. I have no agenda at all except to seek truth and to accept it, however galling it may be. I can only observe and call the shots like I see them. If new evidence arrives to change that view, I'll change it, but the fact that good or bad people think some of the same thoughts is unpersuasive.

I do not say that only vices are human nature. All virtues are, too. The angry chimp showdown is usually followed by conciliatory grooming. Both are chimp nature, aggression and reconciliation.

You say I must "pluralize" my thought, but, Charles, I have multiplexed my thought to include every single thing all at once. I suggest it is you who are thinking narrowly. When you reduce the world to millions of little things and learn how to juggle them, you imagine yourself to be highly pluralistic. All of those little things are just parts of one big thing. They are mere ciphers of a great equation. It's the equation that tells the sum. In a number thousands of places long, what does it mean if you can muscle a digit in the tens column.

Your young, non-utopian universalist friend,
DW

10

Breakfast with the Beatles

September 21, 2003

Dear Charles,

It's Sunday morning, and, as on every Sunday, I'm listening to "Breakfast with the Beatles" on the radio. It runs from 9 till 11 weekly. It has, in addition to regular Beatles fare, rehearsal tracks, live performances, interviews, and a sample of the most excellent and imaginative covers of Beatles tunes by other bands. I never was a big Beatles fan when they were together. But I appreciate them more and more these days. Their musicianship is so far above that of modern popular bands it's ridiculous; their lyrical ingenuity and sly humor exceeds anything of this day. Listening to the show is one of the habits I've developed since coming here. We are creatures of habit, aren't we? It's one of the ways we try to impose order on the chaos of existence.

I finished Bob Fogelin's *Walking the Tightrope of Reason*. It was excellent: great style, lucid, and persuasive. But he has an underlying sentiment which shows through in several places and causes him to gloss over some vectors within the dynamic range of his theses. First, I want to talk about a tightrope as a metaphor. On the one hand I like it because I believe pure logic is just that tricky to stay balanced upon; and it's just that easy to fall. I don't like it because, unlike a real tightrope, those who step off the tightrope of reason don't fall and splatter on the pavement below. Often they keep right on walking—three blocks astray—and have a horde of followers walking devoutly on the same thin air behind them. This is why I constantly remind myself that belief and truth are not the same. We all believe our beliefs are true. The forces of selective distortion and selective retention are relentless, even in the lives of sober thinkers. So I mistrust reason.

Transcendent Reason—Truth—is but an ideal. In the real world, reason is the servant of belief—its ill-used prostitute. If that's not the case, tell me how many times some reasoned "Truth" has swept a tide of profound change across the world as opposed to how many times raw faith felled and raised whole civilizations. Reason in the hands of humankind is like a little red dog panting on the lap of the Infinite Imagination of the Collective Unconscious.

I hope you and Zelda are well. I'm enjoying the books I ordered. Next time I'm ordering two Atlases of the World, Rand McNally and a Hammond.

Until next time,
DW

October 5, 2003

Dear Charles,

"Breakfast with the Beatles" time again. Thought I'd write to tell you the news: I'm scheduled for oral arguments in the 7th Circuit Court sometime this month. They should rule in two to six months. Two to six months after that I'll be dead. It's surprising to me how comfortable I am with that.

Something happened this week that made me remember a great example of why I mistrust "reason." Check out this quote:

> Man cannot survive except by gaining knowledge, and reason is his only means to gain it. Reason is the faculty that perceives, identifies and integrates the material provided by his senses. The task of his senses is to give him the evidence of existence, but the task of identifying it belongs to his reason, his senses tell him only that something is, but what it is must be learned by his mind. . . . In the name of the best within you, do not sacrifice this world to those who are its worst. In the name of the values that keep you alive, do not let your vision of man be distorted by the ugly, the cowardly, the mindless in those who have never achieved its title. Do not lose your knowledge that man's proper estate is an upright posture, an intransigent mind and a step that travels unlimited roads.

This is spoken by a character in a book that profoundly impressed me in 1975, when I read it in prison. The character's name is John Galt, and he is espousing the ultimate philosophy of unsullied Reason and unadulterated Individualism: Objectivism, Ayn Rand's legacy.

I saw the book on the book cart and reread it. I was not nearly as impressed as before. I'm sure you're familiar with Ayn Rand. Her philosophy caught fire in the '60s. Ironically, since it espouses individualism, a sycophantic cult rose up around her calling itself "The Collective." She was once asked by a reporter if she could define Objectivism, and she is said to have replied:

1. Metaphysics: Objective Reality
2. Epistemology: Reason
3. Ethics: Self-interest
4. Politics: Capitalism

Thus, reality exists independent of human thought. Reason is the only viable method for understanding reality. Every person should seek personal happiness and exist for one's own sake, and no one should sacrifice himself or be sacrificed for others. Laissez-faire capitalism is the political-economic system in which the first three best flourish.

Her philosophy is the opposite of the relativism of left-leaning intelligentsia, which pretends to believe there are no absolutes, except you're absolutely wrong to disagree with them. Rand taught that knowledge and moral absolutes are attainable through reason. If your reasoning is flawed it can be corrected. If you don't correct it you are "wrong headed." Not, "I disagree." Just, "You are wrong."

I'm not saying that relativism is right, that all values are essentially equal. I think truth is often a great 3-D phenomenon. If I study an elephant's ass and you study his trunk, our conclusions will be different. Our crime is not being wrong, but that our knowledge is incomplete.

I'm not even an 8th grade graduate. I'm not trained to express philosophical ideas, so I often feel I miss making my point. *Atlas Shrugged* made me see an opportunity to better illustrate a recurring theme of my letters.

Curiously, ironically, I am trying to give a reasoned explanation of my distrust of reason.

Enough for today. I hope you and Zelda are well in spirit and health.

DW

October 10, 2003

Dear DW,

Your October 5 letter knocked the wind out of me. My first impulse was to look for a chance to spend that day driving to the prison. Zelda volunteered to go too. But I had an appointment in Indianapolis with the brace maker, and we had other commitments.

I enjoyed the quote from Ayn Rand. I never read her books, and none of our friends discussed her ideas. I just knew that she wrote books on the bestseller lists, and had a following of some kind. I must have seen the movie based on one of her books. (Wasn't Gregory Peck in it?) I thought the quotation was inspirational and understand that it must have impressed you when you were in prison 28 years ago. You were a teenage prisoner whose behavior was evidently not influenced by the message of the novel. There, I think, is a mystery. Why didn't Ayn Rand turn you around? People say "XYZ changed my life." Can a church sermon, a college course, a book really change someone's life?

I was flattered after giving a lecture at a meeting in Tokyo when a young man came up to me and said, "You changed my life when I took your course in medical anthropology at Berkeley." I didn't recognize him at first (the course had nearly 100 students), but then I remembered that he had consulted me about medical schools where he might continue his interest in anthropology. He finished medical training and was in Japan on some project. A little later I overheard him say to someone else, "You changed my life . . ." A line every teacher would love to hear, but after that I was less flattered.

I am puzzled why you think that I or other "do-gooders" think we can solve all human problems. I never felt that I had any perceptible influence on the large issues in our society, or even on our own children. In old age I have been surprised to realize what wonderful children we have: hard working, liberal minded, against war and for preserving the environment. If they are like their parents in some respects, they are almost totally different from me personally. My wife must have been the persuasive parent in our family. In other primates, too, the mother is the key influence on the character of offspring.

> With great concern for you, I am yours truly,
> Charles

October 15, 2003

Dear Charles,

Thanks for the recent letter and the $. I just wanted to write a quick note to answer your question about attending the oral arguments at the 7th Circuit. Honestly, I have no idea whether or not the public can attend. They're set for the afternoon of either October 22 or 23. I forget which. I have only two issues, both on sentencing, and they're "law professor" questions, technical and obscure. The most I could get from them is a new sentencing hearing. Since I'm quite ambivalent about which is better, to die soon or live a slow death forever imprisoned, the issues are of no interest to me. There is little or no chance I'll win anything in the 7th Circuit. I didn't mean to upset you. I'll be around for awhile.

As for Ayn Rand's "inspiring quote," it was all horseshit. The Collective was a cult with her as the Goddess. She was just another would-be Messiah, bending reason to her views.

Until next time,
DW

October 24, 2003

Dear DW,

We are going to Boston on November 6 to see how our son has renovated the house he bought, and we will celebrate my 80th birthday with friends in Cambridge. Our children and grandchildren will gather in St. Louis for Thanksgiving. Immediately after that we go to London for 9 days, and then will attend a conference on Ayurveda at Cambridge University. We have a very full plate until Christmas, which we will celebrate quietly in Bloomington.

The Bloomington paper has an article today on the prison you are in, saying that health inspectors have cited unsanitary conditions and that a court has ordered prison officials to clean the place. The complaints that led to the inspection came from the death row prisoners. I will enclose the clipping from the *NY Times* about a Human Rights Watch report on mental illness in U.S. prisons.

Yours,
Charles

November 4, 2003

Dear DW,
We think about you every day. Quakers say that they hold a person
in the light. They pray, believing in a personal God who listens to
them and decides whether or not to respond to them. I don't pray for
you, but hold you in the light by remembering your situation and
wishing there was something I could do about it.
We voted a straight Democratic ticket this morning for local officials. Somehow we maintain the conviction that how we vote makes a
difference.
The protagonist in George Orwell's *1984* attended a movie where
a newsreel showed scenes of the perpetual war the government waged
in remote places. A civilian boat had been sunk and the passengers had
escaped in life rafts. A fighter plane was strafing them as the camera
zoomed in on a mother who threw herself in front of her child to protect it. As bullets ripped through her body the audience broke into
laughter at the ineffective absurdity of her gesture.
What can we do to resist the world's brutality? I think we must, like
the mother, preserve our humanity with futile gestures. But the futility
is sometimes overwhelming and I lapse into passivity.
I am about to write something sentimental and stupid, like "but the
world is also beautiful." In fact, I think, when I am reasonable, that
the world is indifferent. "Reality," whatever that is, is indifferent to
our wishes.

Peace,
Charles

November 16, 2003

Dear Charles,
Greetings friend. I guess one of the benefits of academia is that you
get to meet a lot of interesting people. When you told me about your
30th birthday party in Cambridge with academic friends you have
known for years it seemed to me that you've spent your life with interesting people. I spent most of my life with thieves, dope fiends, prostitutes, and other outlaws.
You expressed surprise that I'm liberal in some areas and conserva-

tive in others. I don't like unrestrained or laissez-faire capitalism. I would implement many ideas to restrain capitalism. I would legalize drugs, prostitution, and gambling. Anyone could say whatever he liked, but he wouldn't have much remedy at law if he ran around calling people niggers and got his ass whipped.

The right for people to practice any sort of mutually consensual sex would be protected, provided they were of age. On the other hand, I would have no hate crime laws. I'd punish anyone who assaulted anyone else without direct provocation.

I would immediately stop the sale of arms to other countries. Only disaster and humanitarian causes could loose U.S. coffers of taxpayer's money.

If any public official was caught lying or manipulating public opinion with propaganda, he or she would be stripped naked and publicly flogged. All political campaigns would be run with a small amount of public funds. There would be absolutely no private lobbying. Anyone who subverted the process of legislation like the insurance companies did in the Clinton health care plan would be horrifyingly punished and made to confess their crimes in public.

Peace and love,
DW

November 23, 2003

Dear DW,
Thanks for the November 16 letter about things you would do if you ran the country. You are right, some items sound liberal, but other things in your list sound like the Taliban, e.g., stripping naked an official who lied or manipulated public opinion and subjecting him to public flogging.

Hey, I don't think you really believe in the public flogging of nude liars. Still, it is a delight to contemplate George Bush and his advisors all naked on a stage in a prison courtyard ready to be flogged before a huge invited audience as TV cameras record the event for the rest of the world. Of course, we would have to determine that they lied outright and were not self-deceived, which is just as likely. Would you hesitate to advocate public flogging for self-deception? The consequences might be just as grave, but having deceived themselves the liars would be telling the truth!

Holidays are upon us. We leave two days from now for our St. Louis family gathering, then on to London and Cambridge. I hope when we return we will have a letter with personal news from you. You correspond with a number of people. Who are they? I recall you describing how you wrote your thoughts during meditation and sent them to someone in Oregon. Who is that? How do they respond to what you write? Do you correspond with people you knew in your youth? You are much more isolated from other prisoners now than in Michigan City, but can you communicate with Kevin? How is he? How is your health? I would really like to hear personal news from you.

Peace,
Charles

November 30, 2003

Dear Charles,

Here's the thing that really gets me: you express shock at the idea of public floggings. But no one thinks anything about sentencing people to 100 years in prison. My theory on this is that we best tolerate our national sadism when it's invisible. We can't bear to see ourselves openly as we are. I remember when the Singapore justice system "caned" the 18-year-old American who vandalized several cars. Our media expressed shock and outrage. In prison I wished I could get off with caning. If you came to me on January 1st of each year and offered me a Rodney King ass-whipping in lieu of that year's incarceration, I would kiss your feet and weep tears of gratitude. But it's not about me, is it? It's about "society." Society could see my pain if you beat me. So society chooses the invisible pain and calls itself enlightened and compassionate. I will tell you, though, that physical punishment is far kinder.

We should go back to Michigan City right after the first of the year. It would probably be better to wait until then to visit.

Can I ask a favor? I need a 2004 wall calendar. It will have to come from a bookstore or office supply store directly. We can't receive them from private individuals, like books. Also, it can't be spiral bound. I would like it to have at least 1 $\frac{1}{2}''$ squares for each day so I can keep track of things on it. I write down when I send and receive mail, have visits, receive books, and record things that happen around here. I need a large calendar. Can you help? Also, make sure it has no metal hanger on the back. I think this will be my last calendar.

Tell you the truth, after 24 years of prison, I'm not too sad about the dreamless peace of the grave.

Thanks for not praying for me. That you care is better than prayer.

Until next time,
DW

December 21, 2003

Dear DW,

We got back from England on December 14 and have recovered from jet lag. The conference on Ayurveda at Cambridge University had about 20 participants. I knew most of them, so it was good to see these friends and to meet other scholars for the first time.

I will enclose a copy of the letter that we sent out with Christmas cards this year. When we got back I had your letter of November 30 asking for a calendar. Evidently you mailed it before getting my November 23 letter and the later card with a money order. I bought an astrology calendar that had large squares to record events and had it mailed.

What you write about the cruelty of prison life is moving but does not convince me that executions and violent punishment of any other kind should be made a public spectacle. Every society needs to restrain violence. When there are millions of us, we live for the most part among strangers, and some kind of prison system is necessary. The problem is that the American system should be drastically reduced and the death penalty abolished. Our drug laws are too punitive, our police and court systems often unjust, and we lack adequate governmental and private agencies to help antisocial and otherwise troubled people. All this is well known and people are working to bring about needed changes, but they are impeded by the dead weight of insensitive conventionality.

You ignore my questions about your own activities to write instead about hypothetical things. You write that you will be moved back to

Michigan City soon after the new year. I hope the renovations there have not made it more like the place you are in now.

Yours truly,
Charles

December 2003

Dear Charles,

Hi. Thanks for the letter. I must be losing my mind completely. I had no recollection of asking for an astrological calendar. I don't believe in astrology, not even a little bit. I cannot for the life of me understand why I said that. All I wanted was a large wall calendar with inch and a half squares. I write down daily events on it.

The mail that you inquired about was from two attorneys, my sister (her yearly letter), my niece (a rare letter), and an anti-death penalty activist. No, I haven't a lot of friends from the old days. I've been away for 24 years, many of them are dead, in prison, or still dope fiends.

There is no reality to my life except continual mental agony. Hypothetical stuff is an escape. While you were in England I sat in a 5 by 7 foot cell. Sometimes I paced. Sometimes I watched TV. Sometimes I read. And that is it. That is all forever and ever, year upon year.

You heard nothing I said because you have a "party line" on violence and a sane society. You can't know how violent prisons are. You say we need them. But you know not whereof you speak. This is violence, continual, hopeless, disintegrating the mind. I beg God to let me endure a terrible ass-whipping in trade for even a few months—I beg! But no. God is an evil fucking monster created by this society, which makes no sense to me. Either you've never had an ass-whipping or a prison stay upon which to rest your pithy conclusions, or you don't really care how they compare owing to your views. Makes no difference—you can't know how terribly wrong you are. Violence doesn't have to be visible to be violent. A caning is nothing compared to a year in prison. But you can't hear, I can't tell you, so why try?

That's my Reality. Since you haven't lived it, you get the hypothetical. I know cruelty and violence as you never will—thank God for that. And worse still, how many times have guards beaten me in prison? You have no clue to what prison is. None.

Yesterday I paced for three hours. Tried to daydream, but even old memories fade away. I remember more about prison than life out there. I was 22 when I got locked up. I've been here for 24 years. I tried to read but I was too restless. We are locked down this week for shakedowns. This is stressful because you know you'll lose some of the pitiful little bit you've tried to collect to make your life a tiny bit better. Like always, they come and take it from you. Then they write you up for having contraband and punish you. How dare you try to make your life more livable!

So I was too restless to read. Only seven channels on TV here, two of them don't work well. Nothing on. Didn't feel like listening to radio. Feet and legs tired of pacing. So sat down and suffered in silence. After a couple of hours I was able to pace some more. Mind wanders between dread of the coming shakedown and hope to get it over with. Would have had a cup o' joe but the hot water, which is never really hot, is cold again. It goes up and down all day. Tried to read Jung's *Man and His Symbols*, but my mind was still too restless. I lay down, staring at the wall. Mind drifted through a hodge-podge of memory and worries. Looked at the astrological calendar on the wall and thought that I must be going insane. Have no memory of asking for an astrological calendar. Wonder what possessed me to write that? Wonder if my atrocious script was so illegible that some other word seemed like "astrological." That would be better than being so insane as to ask for something I have no use for. If I did write it, why? What would such a Freudian slip indicate? Sigh. It was only 7 p.m. Hoped I'd get tired soon. Sleep is an escape (perchance to dream!). No luck. Did some pushups and paced again. 8:30 p.m., listened to radio. Grieg's "Hall of the Mountain King" was on WFMT. Listened to that for awhile. Patrolled up and down the dial for awhile. Caught a few songs. Sometimes songs call back memories. Sometimes you wish they didn't. About 9:30 p.m. I paced some more. Read about 30 pages of the Jung book. It wasn't absorbing reading, though. Too much going on. I hate reading half-assed like that. Finally the 10 p.m. news came on. Watched it idly. Tried to watch *Nightline*, topic: "How could intelligence on Iraq's WMD have been so wrong?" But it was the same old stuff, nothing new. Got to bed about 11:30.

That's a slice of my reality. It's more or less the same every day. Every week. Every month. Every year. Every decade. Nothing changes. I talk to my youngest sister every once in awhile. Have no other family relations. No old friends. I just sit in a cell and sit in a cell and sit in a cell and sit in a cell and sit in a cell. And then, I sit in a cell some more after that. Sometimes, early in the morning, I sit in a cell.

Occasionally, I sit in a cell. Eat, breath, shit, sleep, sit in a cell. When I can't stand it anymore and feel as if my ears are bells of ringing madness I sit in a cell.
Sit in a cell
Sit in a cell
Sit in a cell
Sit in a cell
Well, I must go now. I have to sit in a cell. Hope you never have to sit in a cell.

DW

P.S.—Thanks for the calendar and book, but this whole calendar thing spooks me. I may be sitting in a cell too much.

5
The Year 2004

11

Hunger Strike

January 6, 2004

Dear Charles,

I was trying to remember what else you asked besides who had sent me personal mail and why. I can't keep any significant amount of mail here. If I am caught with an amount exceeding the limit it will be seized and I will be punished. So I answer it and toss it.

I think you asked once again about who my "spiritual teachers" or "gurus" were. I don't have any spiritual teacher or guru. I don't believe in them. How can someone else possibly tell me the contents of my soul? My personal unconscious is uniquely mine. So is the way it relates to the collective unconscious. No one else could possibly "teach" me my own soul. If my colleagues taught me anything, it was only how to access my own unconscious. There is no "teaching" beyond this. In fact, most of my associates would kill Buddha if they met him on the path. For the true Buddha is within.

Religion is the most intensely private and personal thing there is for me. I don't care what other people's religious views are. I don't share mine. I did not answer this question because I thought I had spoken on it at length before. I was certain that I'd told you before that I don't have or believe in gurus, so for you to ask about my guru seemed calculated as a provocation or insensitive. So I ignored it. If you were deliberately baiting me, I wasn't going to rise. If you simply disregarded my previously stated disdain for gurus, I wasn't going to rebuke you. I ignored it.

I've also told you before that I had minimal contact with family or old friends. You pick this scab continually. I bleed. But I don't lash out. I just ignore it. Bear it. I have enough trouble maintaining my sanity without the strain of taking umbrage, so I ignore it. Now, however, you challenge me directly about it. So I try to explain. If I say nothing worth your time, you should write to someone else. There are plenty of gregarious fellows around, and I'll put you in contact with one of them if you desire it.

Oh, yes—you asked if I heard from Kevin. I don't hear from anyone. I live in a supermax control unit designed for isolation. If my nearest neighbor and I shout at the top of our lungs we can have a halting conversation. That's it. I live in a cell. If I tell you what I did on any day it would be the same 3 months or a year from now. There is only so much you can do, and in 24 years I've done everything possible 10,000 times. My world is of thought and the "hypothetical" because actions are limited and doomed to repeat ad nauseum and infinitum.

I wish I did have a life full of events and circumstances I could write great letters about, but I live alone in a little steel and concrete box always. It is terrible enough to live this tedious repetition of days. Don't ask me to write it over and over. I don't know what to tell you. I'll bet it frustrates me far more than it does you, though

I am what I am. I have what I have. Would you like someone else's name and number?

Yours,
DW

January 6, 2004

Dear DW,

I look forward to your move back to Michigan City and hope the more liberal visiting arrangements there will still be in effect. However, the renovations may make it as punitive as the Maximum Control Center.

I started work on the lecture I will give in Amsterdam this spring by reading *Bowling Alone* by Robert Putnam. It belongs to a tradition of books that characterize American society. Putnam argues that civil society is created by widespread participation in voluntary organizations like labor unions, churches, fraternal societies, and so on. The people who participate in them get to know each other, form friendships, and take responsible roles in community affairs. This cultivates a general sense of trust in other people and in social institutions. Yet across the board in the United States, membership is declining. The book title refers to the 72 percent decline of participation in the American

Bowling Congress since 1977. The issue is whether as a consequence skepticism and indifference have increased, marking a decline in democratic institutions and the moral order.

I will study Putnam's book and compare it to earlier studies that defined major shifts in American culture. In the 1950s one of my teachers at the University of Chicago wrote a book of this kind called *The Lonely Crowd,* and several decades later a Berkeley sociologist wrote another one called *Habits of the Heart.* I will reread those books. It should be fun.

I saw the doctor a few days ago who audits my prostate cancer once every six months. The antigen blood test called PSA has been climbing over the past decade. He said that it is now at a point where these cancers are likely to metastasize. I opted for no therapy when the cancer was diagnosed in 1991. This is called "watchful waiting," in contrast to "heroic measures," such as surgery or radiation.

Keep me informed about your move back to Michigan City. Are you still studying Arabic? Anything new about the status of your case?

Sincerely,
Charles

January 11, 2004

Dear DW,

The error about the calendar is entirely mine. Before going to buy the calendar I glanced at your letter and misread "2004 calendar" as "Zody calendar" and looked for one with signs of the zodiac. You once mentioned signs of the zodiac in discussing Qabalah.

Your description of the agony of confinement was moving. You are right, I have no experience of your suffering. Can people imagine what they have never experienced? We do it all the time. Your letter made me do it, at a considerable distance from the reality, of course. I hope that the move back to Michigan City will improve your situation.

The calendars at Barnes and Noble are now half price, and there were few to choose from. The new one I bought for you seemed attractive to me. The pictures can be torn off if you don't like them.

I am sorry that you were pissed by the first calendar and by my letters. You write that you have had no spiritual teacher, but you told Zelda and me earlier that a knowledgeable person who was formerly a prisoner introduced you to the Qabalah. You said that he lives in Oregon and that his instruction has been a source of "spiritual alchemy" for you. Once when we visited, you had just shaved your head to undertake an extended period of meditation. You said then that you had been recording your thoughts to send them to someone (we assumed in Oregon) to comment on. Also, since being moved to the supermax you asked me to buy an encyclopedia which you said another prisoner told you was on sale at Barnes and Noble. Thus, you appeared to have some communication with others.

Since my letters have been insensitive to your suffering I hope you will forgive me. I have written to you about my family and what we are doing as I would to people we annually send Christmas letters to. The manner is one that Bronislaw Malinowski, an anthropologist, called "phatic communion," referring to the small talk between people that expresses friendship. Such small talk fills the voids in daily life. I asked about your communication with others—whoever, whatever—in the spirit of phatic communion, with no intention of further wounding you.

Of course, if you wish I will stop writing.

Sincerely,
Charles

January 13, 2004

Dear Charles,

Wow! I have prostate cancer too! Mine was diagnosed three years ago. I declined treatment. If I survived death row I'd probably die of the Hepatitis C I contracted in the late '70s, before anyone even knew what it was. They called it "Non-A/Non-B" back then. Is your prostrate enlarged? I hope you keep hanging in there. Mine is. It's difficult to urinate most of the time, and I miss those days when I could take a long free-flowing piss.

I've noticed what Putnam is talking about. I think that we've all lost faith and trust in our society. Post-modernism and relativism have conditioned many people to accept all values as equally valid. Political correctness intimidates others so that they don't assert independent values.

I'll be glad to get back to Indiana State Prison; even if they've made it a lot worse it still won't be as bad as here.

Yours,
DW

January 16, 2004

Dear Charles

Thanks for yours of the 11th. I'm glad to learn that I didn't ask for an astrological calendar! This one's OK: it meets all the criteria: (1) wall calendar, (2) big squares, (3) no spiral binding. It has astrological information, but I can write over it. Some Qabalists may believe in astrology. I know all the signs, but for me they are only labels under which to file ideas. I gave astrology the fairest possible trial back in the early '80s, but I couldn't find a single bit of evidence to support it.

Ghosts, demons, angels, vampires, sorcerers, magic are all stuff of the unconscious mind, dream stuff. Our minds have conjured such archetypes since time immemorial. They represent a type of truth, a sort of alphabet more primitive than language. It's difficult to describe, but your mind has to shift into a different mode to let visions flow. If you start to observe like a scientist, the visions cease immediately. You can't operate in both modes simultaneously.

This is the real activity of magicians and mystics. Magicians try to use the fruits for power—try to pull back ideas that will help them on earth. Mystics try to cross over and stay as long as they can. Many are called but few stick with it long enough to have that first sustained vision. A vision of this sort is different from the little spontaneous numinous episodes, like feelings of the oneness of everything, the presence of the divine, etc. These may occur to anyone. They may inspire a recipient to endure the tedium and initial lack of any result in meditation to persist long enough to open the Gates of Hell, which are also the Gates of Heaven. They become true Holy Men, but never mistake that for meaning that they are gentle and enlightened beings. A prophet is nearly as likely to lead a genocidal war as he is to give the good law that lifts a people out of chaos. For every Buddha there is a Joshua and eight or so other types as well. A Holy Man is just a man whose thought operates in another mode. There is never a shortage of fools who'll sanctify them and follow their will wherever it leads.

Even when Christ tells us that we are all sons of God and that the Kingdom of Heaven is "within" us we refuse to hear Him. This is why I disdain teachers. All their teaching will be hijacked and involuted and profaned. Long before the New Testament, Holy Men knew "not to cast pearls before swine."

This is all digression, though. I don't know if Qabalists in general believe in astrology as a system to predict events or to divine the natures of persons. I don't believe in it. If other qabalists do, it's on them. I don't care one way or the other.

DW

January 27, 2004

Dear DW,

I have your letter of the 16th. You didn't mention the second calendar I sent with large squares for each day and no astrological information. By now you should have it. Meanwhile, I enclose a money order. Maybe what you buy with it will be a distraction and a bit of pleasure for you.

The last few days we have had lots of snow, which I like very much. It is beautiful and adds to the sense of comfort in being indoors. Walking and driving are made more interesting, too. We lived for 10 years in southern California. When we left I welcomed what people usually call bad weather, vowing that I would never complain about sleet, snow, rain, heat, cold, or whatever.

I am reading other things related to *Bowling Alone* to catch up on neo-Tocquevillian empirical democratic theory. It is interesting to see how a major current debate among political scientists runs along the same lines that divided social scientists 50 years ago, when I was a graduate student:

I enclose a *New York Times* story about the International Court of Justice in The Hague ruling in favor of the Mexican government protesting that it was not informed before the trial of one of its citizens about to be executed in Oklahoma. It turns out that 52 Mexicans are on death row in the United States, and Mexican officials were not informed when they were arrested and tried.

Yours,
Charles

February 15, 2004

Dear Charles,

Still waiting to return to Indiana State Prison. No word of when that will be. Fortunately I've had a good H. P. Lovecraft book to read this week. I've always enjoyed his boundless imagination, and what better place for escapist fiction? Most Lovecraft books must be out of print. Years ago I saw excerpts from two of his sonnet sequences, "Fungi from Yuggoth" and "Dreams from R'lyeh." I'm still asking about them. No one knows if they are in print.

The culmination of the Massachusetts Supreme Court's mandate for gay marriages landed in San Francisco this week. Since you're in Berkeley, you know it well. Everybody's up in arms, and it will become an issue in the '04 elections. These issues are difficult for me because I see both sides. Neither side wants a compromise. Marriage was historically a religious sacrament, an invocation of God to bind the man and woman. In modern society it became almost as much a civil contract guaranteeing certain rights and privileges. It seems obvious to me that the solution is to categorize it: marriage for men and women, civil union for same sex partnerships. But why can't gays partake of the "sacramental" aspect of marriage? Well, because God says homosexuality is wicked. Okay, which of the 7,000 gods said that? The One True God that our enlightened culture worships, as opposed to the silly mythical gods of other religions?

I've lost 20 pounds since I came here. I was 230 lbs when I walked in; I'm 210 now. Unfortunately, I'm still about 20 lbs overweight, but I'm working on it.

You mentioned that the $50 might alleviate some of my suffering. And how! I've ordered 4 new books of the escapist genre, which will transport me to fantastic worlds of "What if?" And I still had $29 left for junk food and goodies. So thanks again.

Be well, you and Zelda,
DW

February 22, 2004

Dear Charles,

We received bad news this week. The Department of Corrections has decided to extend our stay here by 12 to 18 months. I don't believe I have a year to 18 months left to live, so I'll never see my art supplies or musical equipment again. So my skies are dull and dreary and bleak, and hope is a word that falls like a brick in the leaden air of this nightmarish dreamscape. De Sade.

I'll do what I can to endure. It's just a hard blow because we all thought we were getting ready to go back to Indiana State Prison.

I got some new reading glasses, not bi-focal. They're a relief. It's so nice to read without having to look down my nose.

I'm listening to Tommy Dorsey's *Beale Street Blues* right now. Did you ever like that kind of big band music? I like it. Glenn Miller's *In the Mood* was the first of that genre I heard. You've never said if you cared for pop music, except Dylan.

I'm not in a writing mood, so I'll cut this short.

DW

February 26, 2004

Dear DW,

I read about the delay in renovating Indiana State Prison, but thought you would be returned there in June. I am sorry this will not happen.

I just learned that the doctoral oral I will participate in is scheduled for June 15. Now we will start planning the trip. Zelda will leave before I do, going to Italy to stay with her family. I will go directly to Amsterdam. We will meet in Switzerland to visit friends there and in Munich.

I checked the Lovecraft books at Borders (which will not mail books to prisons, but Barnes and Noble, will, and probably has the same ones). They are:

> *The Dream-Quest of Unknown Kadath*
> *The Tomb and Other Tales*
> *Lord of an Invisible World: An Autobiography in Letters*

The Road to Madness: Twenty-nine Tales of Terror
Bloodcurdling Tales of Horror and the Macabre
The Things on the Doorstep
More Annotated H. P. Lovecraft
The Lurker at the Threshold

Do you have a preference among them? I was surprised by the number since I had not heard of him.

My problem with books of this kind is that I am a slow reader, and there are many things in the canon of "great books of Western Civilization" that I still have not read. When I take off from reading anthropology or magazines, I want to read Tolstoy, Camus, Thomas Mann, or classic Greek plays.

I love this gay marriage controversy in a presidential election year. George W just came out with the "protect this sacred institution" statement one expects, and Kerry, like the usual Democratic weasel, advocates civil union, but no marriage for gays. This is in line with his vote supporting Bush's push for the war in Iraq. It will be interesting to see whether this plays out like the race issue. During World War II politicians argued against racial integration, asserting that white and black soldiers could never eat together, sleep and bathe in the same barracks, and so on. Immediately after the war Truman desegregated the military, and it was easily accomplished. Riots and arguments about segregated housing in the 1950s and '60s led to lunch counter sit-ins and refusal to sit in the back of the bus. By the '80s no one in polite society would admit to racism, though they might not let blacks into their country clubs. Now middle- and working-class people agree in public that race prejudice is a bad thing.

Charles

February 29, 2004

Dear Charles,

Hi. Typical Sunday morning. I watch "Sunday Morning" on CBS, then move to the radio for "Breakfast with the Beatles," and letter writing for the week.

As the idea sinks in that we're to be here for another year to 18 months, the more I hope the 7th Circuit will rule quickly against me on my appeal. Six months after oral arguments is the average time. My oral arguments were on October 22, 4 months ago. So it should be soon.

I apologize if I overreacted to your charge that our correspondence was entirely one-sided. It's like routine giving a comforting illusion of choice; I had illusions of being alive. You simply stated the truth: I have nothing left but empty musings. I can't even carry my half of a conversation. I've been dead for years already—have only a semblance of life nowadays. I reacted because I'd been desperately avoiding that reality. But it was just a routine, a way of enduring by force of habit. Now I'm left with only weariness and the self-mockery of my empty pedantry. So, I apologize. Sometimes the truth hurts, and pain makes you lash out. I can't evade any truth once I come to know it.

In any case, things will move quickly once I get a ruling—maybe 60 to 90 days left after that. And I do begin to look at death as, finally, peace. I've felt like the world hated me since I was born, and everything was a continual fight. At this point it doesn't matter how much of that I chose for myself. It's all water under the bridge. I weary of the fray. I want to lay down and sleep forever.

Sorry to end on such a gloomy note, but I can't think of anything else worth talking about.

DW

March 4, 2004

Dear DW,

I got your sad letter yesterday. Zelda and I are sorry for you. That does no good at all, but if there was such a thing as Extra Sensory Perception you could at least have a vague experience of our sympathy.

We were taken out last night to an expensive restaurant. It was crowded and loud. The roar of people shouting at each other and laughing made it impossible to hear others at our table, yet we persisted for almost two hours in trying to carry on a conversation. I nodded and smiled, not having a clue to what people were saying. When the facial expression indicated that an answer was demanded I would lean forward, cup both ears with my hands and ask the speaker to repeat herself. If the devil wanted a hell specially designed for me he could just assign me to another evening in that restaurant.

Hold on! I enclose a money order, just in case it will help a little.

Charles

March 10, 2004

Dear Charles,

Thanks for your latest letter, the $, and your and Zelda's condolences on my bad news. I'm struggling to lift myself out of this depression. Maybe the thought of new books will help.

Your experience at the restaurant sounds like trying to converse with someone here. Anytime you speak, your own voice echoes loudly in the cell, drowning out what the other person is yelling. Of course, you say "What?" and they begin yelling again before the echo dies. Any background noise also drowns out words. It's a frustrating experience. You end up just saying, "Yeah, okay!" The equivalent of your smile and nod when you have no idea what was said.

I'm reading Albert Camus' "The Myth of Sisyphus." He explores how we deal with the absurdity of human life by eluding (finding some principle greater than the self to invest in), or escaping (suicide). He wonders if it is possible to live life for itself, to accept the absurd as irrelevant. I've read it before, but it seems better this time, maybe because of my own confrontation with feelings of futility.

DW

March 15, 2004

Dear Charles

I received your letter with the Lovecraft list. I've marked off those I've read.

We're locked down this week. We were shook down today. My cell is all torn up and I lost a lot of little things that are contraband, but which make life easier. This is the third shakedown this year and it's only March. I hate shakedowns. They always hurt. They always invade. More and more I look foreword to my execution as light at the end of the tunnel. Death row was easy time. But this supermax segregation has done me in. Sad, though, when death looks brighter than a prison. There's supposed to be a demonstration in front of the Department of Corrections office in Indianapolis on April 1st. I doubt it'll do any good, but one can hope.

I'm going to try to put my cell back together. I wonder how many times in 24 plus years I've had guards tear my cell apart and seize anything that made life a little better? Hundreds, at least. You always feel like it's an act of hatred against you. No one suffers hatred without beginning before long to return it. So guys come out of prison with blood in their eye. Nowadays even more, as no one even pretends to try to rehabilitate.

Until next time.
DW

March 25, 2004

Dear Charles,

We've had a hunger strike here since the 17th. I started on that day. Nine more joined on the 19th. We're trying to get the Department of Corrections to abandon its plan to keep us here while they refurbish Pendleton, or to make conditions here tolerable.

I'm doing okay. A little weak, but I can testify that fasting promotes a spiritual mood. I've lost 12 pounds. Was 214, weighed 202 today. Nurse said I should quit because of my high blood pressure and various ailments.

I'm going to soldier on. Got to hold out at least until our supporters demonstrate on April 1st. They already have their permit and have organized things as best they can. Want to give them support as best we can. By the time this weekend is over I'll be under 200 lbs. for the first time since I was 31 years old. That's better than the Atkins diet!

Brain is a little numb, though. Lethargy. But spirit burns brighter. Nothing like a good fight to lift one out of depression. I am not dead. I am fiercely alive.

Later,
DW

March 31, 2004

Dear Charles,

Hi. I've lost 22 pounds in 13 days! I'd like to see someone top that diet plan.

Tell you the truth, I feel like hell. Headaches. Nausea. Dry heaves, and pains in the kidneys. My urine is getting darker and darker, and I realize that this means they are being destroyed by the nitrates building up in my system.

My will is amazing, though! I received commissary that I had ordered before the strike. I gave a few items away to some who had fallen out of the strike, but the rest has been sitting within easy reach. I don't touch it. My hunger transcends itself so that it doesn't even seem like hunger.

Today I was confused for a moment when I awoke—took me a second to realize where I was or what the hell was going on. I don't know how fast or how much this symptom will reoccur, so I'm writing now while I still have my wits.

The 7th Circuit rejected my appeal. I have probably 3 or 4 months left to live anyway. So why not go out like Bobby Sands? At least millions know his name. It would add a great deal of political punch to the efforts of my comrades—dramatize the seriousness of their plight. It would give me control over my death (if only symbolically). Plus, I wonder what is at the bottom of me—iron or air? Steel or stercus? I wonder if I can pull forth the strength and courage to endure a long and agonizing death. I look inside my heart and I think it is there, that I can do it. Plus, even though people hate me as the bad guy and a murderer, everyone respects balls and to-the-death commitment. I think I could win huge points for my comrades. It would give meaning to my death.

Anyway, these are my thoughts. They've been coalescing for awhile, and they begin to condense and shine like something even Constantine might like.

This has really worn me out to sit here and write this. I need to rest. I hope you and Zelda are okay. I'm doing well under the circumstances.

As always,
DW

April 2 and 3, 2004

Dear DW,

Your 3/25/04 letter arrived on the 30th and I started phoning and e-mailing to find out about the demonstration you mentioned. I phoned the Bloomington newspaper and left a message on an answering machine complaining that they had not published anything about the hunger strike. Finally I got information from a Unitarian minister. When a reporter answered the message I left, I complained that the paper had ignored the prison strike, and I described the conditions you are protesting. She did additional research and the next morning the paper had a front-page story. I enclose a clipping, along with one from the *NY Times* on the World Court ruling about foreign nationals on death row in the US.

I had phoned the prison to make an afternoon appointment to visit you but decided to join the demonstration instead. Zelda and I will drive up next week.

It was a small demonstration. Phillip Stroud's mother was very active. A handsome woman with her hair plaited in long African corn braids, she used a battery-operated loud speaker to demand that the Department of Corrections "obey the law" by correcting the treatment of her son and other prisoners.

Our signs protested the booths with a glass wall between a prisoner and his visitor. One of the most upsetting things about the supermax is the inability of prisoners and family members to touch each other. Two signs proclaimed, "I want to hug my son before he dies."

I talked to an attractive young woman who said she was Obadaya's girlfriend. This must be a recent relationship because she did not know about the Supreme Court hearing when I visited with Obadaya's mother.

I talked to Paul McManus's mother at some length. A teenage boy with her was Paul's nephew, his brother's son. He said little but expressed affection for his uncle. It was apparent that the family has suffered greatly. Mrs. McManus told me how terrible it was to see her son manacled in the confined space of the interview booth.

Benny Lee Saylor's brother was there, and we walked with others to the governor's office a block away to leave a letter protesting conditions at the Maximum Control Facility.

The Overstreet family, including two charming little girls, was there with a poster that included a family photograph. They brought bag lunches, which the girls had helped to prepare, and gave extra ones to others at the demonstration. The girls handed out leaflets asking people to write the governor and the Department of Corrections commissioner. No one in the DOC acknowledged our existence on the sidewalk outside their office.

It was a sparkling spring day, with sunshine and a bracing wind. A TV van came by to photograph the demonstration, so we may have made the evening news broadcast. We reached a maximum of 17 adults and three children by noon. We were only a few, but it felt good to be there.

Your March 31st letter arrived describing your difficulties fasting. I hope you drink water with a little salt and sugar in it. I think that this is the way fasting of the kind you are engaged in is done. I don't remember whether I read this in stories about IRA prisoners, or, more recently, about hunger strikes against prison conditions in Turkey. The salt and sugar solution is used to prevent dehydration in cases of cholera, or children with severe diarrhea. Even though your letter considers fasting to death, I believe people who kill themselves this way take the water solution.

Dear DW, I admire your courage and realize that you alone will decide what to do.

In sympathy,
Charles

April 1, 2004

Dear Charles,

What a difference a day makes. Today I received word that those who started the hunger strike have already written a simpering letter to the media explaining that we would all quit the strike on Monday.

What burns me up is that I hated the idea of the strike. I resisted joining, but they asked for my support so I gave it. When I reach the point of giving myself completely to the cause, they bail out.

So I have to unwind myself. It will be hard because I've been on my prayer rug several times a day, fortifying my will. Now this—betrayed by those I'd helped. But that's life.

So no glory, and I suppose I'll have to die a ho-hum death by execution (Bo-o-o-o-ring!).

Just wanted to let you know. Take care,

DW

April 6, 2004

Dear Charles,

Got your letter today. Thanks. Good to hear about the demonstration. Nineteen days without food now. This is difficult. Can't think clear. Sick. Dizzy. Weary. But I can go on indefinitely. Everyone else quit on Monday. I'm not quitting. Can't get any salt or sugar. Besides sugar is food. I'm not "fasting," I'm striking. Kidneys are like knives in my back. But my spirit is good.

DW

April 8, 2004

Dear DW,

Why did you refuse to see us? We drove all morning to get to Westville in time to visit, having made a phone reservation the day before. The officer told us on entering your building that you refused to see us. We were astonished and disappointed. We insisted that she phone to someone to tell you that we were there and our names. She verified your refusal. It was a long day on the drive home wondering, "Why?"

Charles

Letter with no date, written with a shaking had so that words are illegible. Received on April 10, 2004.

Dear Charles and Zelda

I'm very sorry. I couldn't get up from . . . am dizzy. Most (or Not?) . . . now . . . Sorry I couldn't make . . . to . . . you. My . . . are burning. Thank you . . . being my . . .

April 12, 2004

Dear DW,

Thank you for writing to explain why you didn't meet us when we visited last Wednesday. The shaking hand with which you wrote demonstrated your suffering. We think of you frequently, always with great sympathy. I understand that despite the pain, dizziness, and other symptoms, you gain spiritual strength.

Several people who were at the demonstration in Indianapolis have sent me e-mails. It is moving to see the way they express their concern for family members in prison. Everyone I talked to at the demonstration knew about you. The e-mails tell me what they have heard about your condition.

I am tempted to ask you to give up your fast, but this would be wrong. Whatever you do, Zelda and I support.

Let us know if you decide to go off your fast. Meanwhile, we send you our regards and deep respect.

Charles

Letter on lined paper in a shaking hand, with sentences slanted down the page, but fairly legible.

April 18, 2004

Dear Charles,

Thank you for your support. I hope you and Zelda can forgive me for . . . visit. I'm sorry. I'm . . . pain. Can't think sometimes. Good visions though. Maybe some progress. They put a bunch of new stuff on commissary. Sausages Cheeses Good Stuff. Makes my mouth water. But I . . . to hold on. Focus my power. I hurt. But I'm learning to be . . . that pain instead of against it. Sorry. Got to Go.

DW

April 20, 2004

Dear DW,

We wonder whether you had to be hospitalized: to save your life, of course, so that the state can kill you later on. You may be recovering from your fast. If you can write, please do.

Meanwhile, I write about myself. Maybe that will distract you. I have been conflicted for months about going to Amsterdam for the Ph.D. oral examination. I advised the student who has completed a study of pharmaceutical companies that produce Ayurvedic and Unani medicines. The university will pay my travel and hotel expenses, so I agreed to give the lecture that I wrote you about.

Meanwhile we have written to arrange visits with friends. The amount of walking such trips involve is more extensive than puttering about the house or driving to a concert in Bloomington. I am likely to damage my foot and then have to supplement the leg brace with crutches. When you don't use crutches often, they are tiring.

I think, Who am I kidding? The trip will be exhausting and my lecture will be an embarrassing flop. Don't misunderstand this lament. I am flattered by the invitation and proud of past accomplishments, but I am a realist. My scholarly days are over, except as a consumer. I enjoy reading the new research.

Let us know about your fast, and how you managed to stay on it for such a long time. If there is a way for us to help you, please let us know.

Charles

April 20, 2004

Dear Charles and Zelda,

I hit the wall at day 31. I'd gone as far as I could. They have me on clear liquids still. Tomorrow I get soft foods and on the 23rd back to regular. My mind is still not fully operational. My body is weak. I lost 39 lbs in 31 days. I'm glad I did it. In the last days I was having florid visions. I was so out of it that I can't recall them wholly, but the impressions are with me still. They gave me great hope in a way.

I've been feeling terrible about how you must have felt to drive all the way here and I couldn't make it. I'm so sorry for that. Your letters show understanding, but I keep thinking of how that must have felt at the time.

I'm still weak and tired. I'll write again soon.

DW

April 25, 2004

Dear Charles,

Hi. I'm almost fully recovered from the hunger strike, except for my kidneys. They hurt like hell. My urine is very dark. The nurses do blood tests and collect urine samples frequently. They say my kidneys may be permanently fried. I couldn't believe how much pain they produced.

I don't know how I lasted 31 days. I wasn't even in my right mind for at least a week. It seems like a dream. I'm glad I did it, but I wouldn't do it again.

I don't know what to say about Holland. I think a lot of talented people have that kind of doubt and fear. Maybe it's because talent is a gift that one does nothing to deserve. Since you can't explain it, you feel like you're faking it.

I felt really down before the hunger strike. I don't think the strike accomplished anything politically. Yet I feel strangely good about the affair—renewed somehow. Maybe it's just good to have something to overcome in life.

Hi Zelda,
DW

May 6, 2004

Dear DW,

This is just a note to send you the enclosed money order. Have a feast on tortilla chips, fig bars, etc. from the commissary. My favorite would be Snickers. We keep a few little ones in the fridge.

Thanks for the encouragement on Amsterdam. In the past I always wrote a complete text for lectures of this kind, but even when you read slowly and with as much expression as you can muster, papers of this length are tedious to listen to. Everyone now speaks in an extemporaneous manner in PowerPoint lectures. PowerPoint has taken the place of "slide lectures." You put a detailed outline of each segment of your talk on a CD, along with charts, graphs, maps, and photographs. This is projected like slides used to be, but you don't have to worry about a slide getting stuck in the projector, or having been put in upside down.

My daughter gives PowerPoint lectures and volunteered to make the CD for me.

This war has been amazing: first the military stood around and did nothing to stop the looting that wrecked the Baghdad infrastructure after we bragged about targeting bombs to keep it intact. There was the collapse of our primary excuse for the war when no weapons of mass destruction could be found. The military plans made no provision for organized resistance to the occupation. Then Bush dressed up like a fighter pilot to land on an aircraft carrier and declare himself a winner under a "Mission Accomplished" banner. Now we see astonishing photographs of American military guards tormenting prisoners at Abu Ghraib while talking heads on TV discuss it without mentioning its context, the long-standing, out-of-sight violation of prisoner rights in Guantanamo.

Yours,
Charles

(no month or day) 2004

Dear Charles,

Hi. Thanks for your note and the money order. I'm a big Snickers fan, too! I usually order 4 or 5 when I turn in a commissary order. I'll toast you and Zelda when I eat my next one!

I feel much better these days mostly because the 7th Circuit ruled against me. It was such a relief to know that my suffering is almost at an end.

The prisoner abuse fiasco is something. If there'd been no cameras, the military would have said, "We don't do that kind of stuff!" Everyone would have believed it.

In Indiana prisoners are often stripped and made to stand around naked, sometimes for hours, sometimes while in handcuffs, often in front of women or under surveillance cameras. We're made to bend over and spread our cheeks often. If you refuse or resist, you'll be shocked, or maced, or beaten into submission. Here at MCC they have a device called "the chair." It half seats and half lays you into a rack-like position, and you're bound to it at the wrists, ankles, waist and chest. The usual dose is 4 hours.

The worst torture is all the mental things they do to you. They leave no marks that anyone can see, but your soul is scarred. You get no sympathy or scarcely even belief that anything was done to you. This intensifies the pain. If you had a black eye, they'd say, "Oh! I bet that hurt; it's outrageous that they beat you like that!" You would trade the invisible wounds for a thousand black eyes. Physical pain is transient, it only affects your shell, and you soon forget it. Your soul never heals, and it is you. You have a place of refuge inside, its name is dissociation. In times of stress it makes you able to kill without malice or sympathy. Prison creates cold-blooded killers. That frightens people so they urge jailers to be harsher and more punitive. If we attempt to explain, no one believes us. Where are the scars? Where are the photographs?

This is why I went nuclear when you proposed that prisons were necessary. I shouldn't have been so incendiary. How can you know what prison really is? How could you believe what it is? How can I articulate it? You can never know what it means to live a year in a supermax prison. If there'd been no pictures in Iraq there'd be no abuse.

What is violence? To you it's a public flogging that leaves red welts that'll heal in a week. To me it's the hidden cuts that scar the soul forever. It drives you insane because people can't see it. You keep hurting and hating and heating up, and then one day they come and say, "You're paroled, see yah!" If the idea of prisons is necessary, the reality of them isn't. They create more evil than they cure.

The war in Iraq has been amazing for the reasons you cited. It is a bumbling fiasco because ideologues are in charge. Only those who doubt their own views can look at possibilities outside those views. Ideologues never doubt, never see beyond their own limited vistas. The sad thing is, people elect ideologues because they appear strong and confident.

Godspeed,
DW

June 18, 2004

Dear Charles,

I hope that you and Zelda enjoyed your trips. I'm doing well. The 7th Circuit has not ruled on my petition for rehearing yet, so that means I have to remain in the world at least until after October. But I don't feel too badly about the delay since I know that peace is in sight.

I've been thinking a lot lately. It seems to me that people have an ideal self—the image of the person they'd like to be—and an actual self that often falls short of the ideal as it deals with the vagaries of existence. Just as the body has automatic responses to heal injuries, the brain has automatic systems to heal mental wounds. Maybe we were cowardly when our ideal is bravery; maybe we lied when our ideal is honesty; maybe we were selfish when our ideal is generosity— whatever. Each time we touch that memory a sort of pain signal goes out, and the automatic responses kick in. We suppress the memory, or we re-image it again and again until it plays back more like the ideal. We edit until we can say, "I'm a good person." This is not the place to discuss the myriad types of editing that may occur. That we create and ingrain fictions to create livable pseudo-realities is enough. By extension, what is true of individuals is true of societies. For example, when Bush says that Abu Ghraib is "not the America I know," he means that it isn't the ideal we project for ourselves, but we are what we do. When exposed, we claim our ideal is who we really are while we continue the same bad behavior.

Everything you see in politics is an extension of playground antics. "Step across this line!" "Do what I want or I won't be your friend anymore." "He started it!" No one in power admits blame or error. Instead they set loose legions of apologists to "characterize" things, "spin" them as something other than what they are. We live in a world of manufactured pseudo-realities, and many of us don't even glimpse this fact. Others see it, but choose from the same compulsion to deny it, or explain it away.

I watch, knowing I can never belong, and if I could I would not.

Cubs baseball is coming on and I try not to miss a televised game.

Until next time.
DW

June 28, 2004

Dear DW,

Your letter was here when we returned. In it you identify a dialectic between ideal and actual selves in which forgetting and edited memories heal the pain of personal failure. I agree that something like that operates in the realm of politics when the president asserts that torture at Abu Ghraib was not American despite the fact that we did it. Now we are learning that government lawyers guided the decision to declare prisoners of war enemy combatants and hold them in Cuba where the techniques used at Abu Ghraib were perfected. Clearly, the American treatment of prisoners was planned with lawyers who justified torture, including also turning prisoners over to countries where we know they will be tortured.

Zelda had a grand visit with her family, and I enjoyed the doctoral oral and other events in Amsterdam. My lecture was OK, not brilliant, but not a disaster either. I haven't done any real research in 20 years, and since moving here have published only an article and a couple of book reviews. Two years ago in Arizona I was introduced to an anthropologist in his mid-40s who was surprised because he thought I was dead.

Being old must be a little like being black. When I meet people for the first time I sometimes notice that my age registers negatively in their eyes. It is a small wound, but I, too, have an instinctive preference for youth and beauty, which appear to be the same thing when you are old. Young people in the Bloomington audiences for classical music increase the pleasure of attending.

I am glad the 7th Circuit court has not ruled on your petition. The world is full of surprises. No one knows what will happen between now and October, and for my part I would prefer you to stay alive.

I am glad, too, that you are resigned to death. It is our common destiny. I am reading a book on Jewish eschatology that opens with this quotation from a Yale physician, Sherwin Nuland: "A realistic expectation . . . demands our acceptance that one's allotted time on earth must be limited to an allowance consistent with the continuity of the existence of our species. Mankind . . . is just as much a part of the ecosystem as is any other zoological or botanical form, and nature does not distinguish. We die so that the world may continue to live. We have been given the miracle of life because trillions upon trillions of living things have prepared the way for us and then have died—in a sense for us. We die, in turn, so that others may live. The tragedy of a single individual becomes, in the balance of natural things, the triumph of ongoing life." I like that because it places individual death in proper evolutionary context, and, I suppose, because I am within spitting distance of my own end.

Hold on,
Charles

July 15, 2004

Dear Charles,

I just got your card from Holland on Tuesday. I've always wanted to visit Amsterdam. I've had several Dutch pen-pals, so I know a lot about their social policies.

Thanks for the $50. I spent all of it on art supplies, which they're finally letting us purchase. It pisses me off, though, because I had to waste money to get basic supplies that I already have at ISP, and stuff is so expensive that I couldn't get all I wanted. It took me years to build up my supplies.

The 7th Circuit finally ruled on my rehearing—denied on June 30. After all these years I'm certain of one thing: death is a lighter sentence than life without parole. Although the death penalty is probably bad for our society, I'm glad people haven't figured out which is worse. They're letting me avoid decades of misery in their lust for blood. God bless them! But you make a profound mistake: I am not "resigned" to death. I yearn for it with all my heart. It's not about a philosophical awareness of the continuity of life and nobly realizing my place in the universe. Death is my only escape from this hell. I yearn for it. Nevertheless, I do like the aesthetic quality of the quote you sent by Sherwin Nuland.

Do you think we'll ever attain a society where justice seeks to reunite malefactors with the community? Will we have a people to whom the idea of war is utterly repugnant? 70 percent of the people at one time supported this Iraq war. It was not repugnant to them,

Peace and love to you and Zelda,
DW

August 8, 2004

Dear DW,

It was good to see you last Monday. I think that the stress of the fast added a few years to your face—wrinkles around the eyes that were not there before—but your weight looked good, and you were animated. I should apologize for getting restless during the last hour. I have a bony ass so that a hard chair becomes uncomfortable after awhile. We were glad that we stayed nearby overnight so that we could make it to the prison in the morning.

I have been reading Bill Clinton's autobiography with pleasure, though it is not a good book. He constructs a simple chronological narrative of his family and what he did and the people he came to know over the years. He concludes a chapter about his high school years by saying, "I liked my life a lot." He wrote that after describing an alcoholic stepfather who mistreated the mother he adored. In Clinton's eyes his mother was a beautiful, fun-loving, and hard-working woman. He repeatedly praises her. He was also attached to his maternal grandfather, who had a small grocery store. His grandfather extended credit to and taught Bill to respect their mostly black customers. These two people were sources of his remarkable self-confidence, gregarious character, and ambition.

I enclose a money order. Buy some Snickers, or whatever.

Yours,
Charles

12

Notes from Underground

August 15, 2004

Dear Charles,

Hi. I enjoyed our visit. No need to apologize for your restlessness at the end of the visit. I am familiar with pain that's aggravated by trying to sit too long. You noticed the new wrinkles? They sure pile up. I hate this place so much that my entire life is soured. I want to die to escape this place. Its effects wear me down. I was generally cheerful before we were moved here, but now I just want to die and be done with it.

I don't want to read Clinton's autobiography. I liked him. He was handsome, charming, and charismatic, but he left the campaign trail to oversee the execution of Ricky Rudd, a man who was so mentally deficient that he told friends to save the rest of his pie for him so he could eat it when he got back from being executed. He pushed and passed the terrible Anti-terrorism and Effective Death Penalty Act in the wake of the McVeigh bombing. This has so stripped the writ of habeas corpus of purview that it is no more than a rest stop on the road to execution. He signed into law the Prison Litigation Reform Act, which makes it almost impossible for a prisoner to effectively litigate abuses or to have real relief if he does win a suit. I and my friends suffer daily because the AEDPA makes it much easier to execute us and because of the PLRA we have to endure prison conditions that we wouldn't have had under Ronald Reagan.

When all is said and done, though, two Clintons would be more tolerable than one Bush. I pine for an Upton Sinclair to come driving up in a Tucker automobile! Then, at least, we'd have something different to complain about.

Have you ever read Dostoyevsky's *Notes from Underground?* I'm reading it now. I suspect you wouldn't like it because its hero hits hard against the ideas of positivism in that era which held that all human

8/15/04

Dear Charles:

Hi. I enjoyed our visit, too. No need to apologize for your restlessness at the end: I beginning to become all too familiar with continual pain that's aggravated by no more than trying to sit for too long. You noticed the new wrinkles? They sure pile up. I hate this place so much that my entire life is soured — I want to die to escape this place. Its effects wear me down. I was generally cheerful at ISP. But every day here is a trial. I just want to die & be done with it.

I probably wouldn't want to read Clinton's autobio. I liked Clinton. He was handsome, charming, & charismatic. 🌹 I ~~also~~ liked his apparent liberal ideology too. But he left the campaign trail to oversee the execution of Ricky Rudd — a man who was so mentally deficient that he told friends to save the rest of his pie for him so he could eat it when he got back from being executed. He pushed & passed the terrible "Anti-Terrorism & Effective Death Penalty Act" in the wake of McVeigh. This has so stripped the writ of habeas

1. Page 1 of letter, August 15, 2004.

ills were the result of disorder and irrationality and that they could be corrected by an exercise of reason. I like the protagonist because he's profoundly alienated and tormented by a brooding self-analysis in a search for truth in a world of relative values. I identify with him. This work if you're interested is included in *White Nights and Other Stories*, the Macmillan Co., New York, 1918.

I hope you and Zelda are well.

DW

August 23, 2004

Dear DW,

Notes from Underground is a classic novella. I used it once as one of the assignments in a course. I thought it would be difficult for Delaware students, but they liked it. Since you identify yourself with the protagonist I will read it again.

I will send you *The Brothers Karamazov*. Dostoyevsky wrote it shortly after he wrote the novella, and the underground theme appears in it as well.

Yours,
Charles

September 6, 2004

Dear Charles,

I can't believe how quickly this year is passing. I've been here for 19 months now.

I would like to read *The Brothers Karamazov*. I intended to purchase it from the Dover Thrift Editions, but they quit doing business with prisoners.

It's the same old thing here: sit in a cell all day every day. I am doing better now that I have some art supplies, though. Drawing is relaxing. I wish I had my guitar, but I can forget that!

My attorney, Sarah Nagy, has to cut back on her work due to illness. She wrote to tell me that she won't be able to do my clemency hearing

She's a good person, and I hope she survives long. I wasn't going to have a clemency hearing anyway. I'm not going to beg for my life. Not only would that be unseemly, I'm so weary of doing time that the grave looks like bliss to me. So no clemency, please!

Take care, friend (Hi Zelda)
DW

September 24, 2004

Dear DW,

I found my copy of *Notes from Underground*. I thought part 1 was tedious when I read it years ago. The narrator's attitude and criticism of reason comes across at once, but he goes on for 30 pages when 10 pages would have made the point as well. The character is brilliantly imagined: his intelligence and neurotic self-understanding, his envy and hatred of others while at the same time he wants to be accepted by them. He fluctuates between self-assertion and humiliated groveling, which he calls his "intellectual and moral vacillation and inaction."

Existentialists in my youth criticized reason, and talked about life grounded in faith. For secular existentialists, in contrast to Dostoyevsky, it was a godless faith. A common argument was that since knowledge is always limited, any significant act requires an absurd "leap of faith." I sympathized with this argument, as anyone moved by 19th- and 20th-century romanticism would do. It assumes as you do, that reason and emotion are incompatible, while I believe that our ability to reason is grounded as much in emotions as it is in logic.

We respond to the narrator's account of his envy and spiteful acts, along with his fear of being insulted and his sense of ineffectualness because it recalls our own experience of these things. Who has not suffered insults or been envious and spiteful? Similarly, we recognize in ourselves the narrator's assertion that people act irrationally and against their own best interests.

The narrator was a particular man in a particular culture. He had been an orphan with no inheritance, a bookish boy shipped off by relatives to a military academy in 19th-century tsarist Russia. Some cadets were from wealthy families and most of them had better social prospects than he had. They treated him badly, but he was committed to the aristocratic life they represented. He wanted to be accepted by people who wore fine clothes and who when insulted challenged each other to a duel. His bitter misery was due to his failure to achieve their life style. His virtue was that he was not sentimental and was thus objective about himself. His objectivity makes it possible for the reader to sympathize with him. It makes this anti-hero heroic.

Now, what do you think of my analysis? I wish I could remember the course I used it in. I read somewhere that as one ages the brain shrinks. At least it doesn't hurt, I don't feel a thing. Continued on September 28

This letter did not address your identification with the narrator of *Notes*. It seems wrong headed to me. You were moved by the novella more deeply than I was. It is, of course, a great work of art. I should have asked you to tell me about its meaning for you. You only wrote that you identified with a narrator. I have imagined your youth differently: as a boy who was certain of himself, smart, cocky. Scornful of others, yes. Angry, yes. But not hung-up on emulating upper-class kids or being accepted by them.

Yours,
Charles

September 25, 2004

Dear Charles,

How are you? I haven't heard from you in a while.

I'm preparing for Ramadan. I've signed up and been okayed to participate. I don't care for Islamic orthodoxy, but the Sufis are cool. They look to the love and mercy of God, whereas the orthodoxy seems to dwell on the wrath and severity. Not always, but too much for me. I like the discipline of fasting and praying during Ramadan. It starts October 16.

I'm not reading anything of note lately—sci-fi escapist stuff, which I love! I'm in the Columbia Encyclopedia you bought me all the time. I've got a lot of joy from that book. I'll look up one thing and end up reading for an hour or more.

Hope you and Zelda are well,
DW

October 19, 2004

Dear Charles,

Greetings. Thanks for the copy of *The Brothers Karamazov*. I won't read it for a while, but it makes me feel good to know I have a good book waiting for me.

I agree with your analysis of *Notes from Underground*. I found the first part tedious and almost put it down, but the narrator grew on me. I identified with him for being honest. Although he condemned people around him, he admitted that he was just as guilty.

I wonder about your statement that "reason is grounded in emotions as much as it is in logic." It seems to me that emotion is the antithesis of reason, a bar to it. If I have bitter hatred and anger against someone, I may soundly reason that he should be killed. If I love someone I may reason that he shouldn't be punished, even when he did something worse than what I have done. Emotion poisons reason. Reason is grounded in logic; sentiment is grounded in emotion. Yet I grant that most of what passes for reason is no more than emotionalism given an excuse. Just because someone can refine that practice doesn't elevate it to "reason." That's nonsense! Poppycock! Piffle! Rubbish! (Actually, I just like a chance to use those comic English exclamations. What is "piffle" anyway?)

I think about how I'm going to be at the end. The dying point will be easy. Death is no more than an inconvenience since there are books I won't get to read, movies I won't get to watch, etc. What will be hard is how everyone will want to visit in the end, especially "family" I haven't heard from in years. It will all be awkward for me, and stressful. I have nothing to say to my father. Yet he will be an exuberant portrayer of sorrow, false to his toenails, never to be swayed from a performance. I think my mother has enough malice in her to stay away, and I'm grateful for that. Others may claim they want "to be there for me." But I don't want anybody holding my hand. Why weren't they "there for me" when I lived? I'd be happy to die in a room surrounded by enemies or by the indifferent.

Peace and love to you and Zelda,
DW

November 14, 2004

Dear DW,

It was good to see you on the 11th. You appeared at ease. When you told us that you were enjoying doing nothing and letting your mind wander it seemed that you were experiencing the calm of knowing that you are reaching the end of a struggle. It may be like arriving finally at the end of a career, as I did some time ago. I looked across the breakfast table and said to Zelda with some satisfaction, "This is it, this is all there is, there isn't any more." A way of saying that we had nothing to look forward to—no promotion, no children to raise, no research grant to write or conference to attend, no future to worry about. I spent my life thinking: when I grow up, when I go to college, when I get out of the army, when I take the exam, when I graduate, when I get the job, when the child is born, when I get another job, when the book is published, when I get promoted, when I get the research grant, and so on year after year until, *This was it, this was all there was, there wasn't any more.* It wasn't a good feeling, but it wasn't bad either. It was just a fact of a certain kind of life preoccupied with the future, with taking the next step. That life was over. Death would no longer interrupt anything; it would be an acceptable ending any time now.

Dear DW, what can I say? Our hearts are with you. You demonstrated strength of will and moral integrity in the fast earlier this year, and you have shown courage in maintaining a spiritual and intellectual life during many years in prison. Your letters and our prison visits have shown us your dignity. Nothing can take that away from you.

Sincerely,
Charles

December 5, 2004

Dear DW,

We think about you every day. Last Monday you were to hear about the final court decision. If things go as you explained them to us, you will be waiting for the execution schedule. I wonder when you will be moved back to Michigan City.

I do pray for you, despite knowing that no God listens. A short prayer, "Oh, God, help him endure." Maybe this is magic. Malinowski said that although Trobriand Islanders had considerable knowledge and practical skills in gardening and fishing, there was still uncertainty about what the outcomes would be, so they used magical spells to supplement their labor. He meant that to apply to all of us.

Charles

December 12, 2004

Dear Charles and Zelda,

Hi. The last two weeks have been hectic. Attorneys keep calling and visiting. To go to the phone I have to suit up in "trip gear"—handcuffs enclosed in a black box that holds them in one position and covers them so they can't be "picked." A chain goes through the box, gets wrapped around your waist, then padlocked—the tail of the chain to the part looped around you—and shackles. It is a pain in the ass to get in and out of only to find that the attorneys have nothing of substance to say, but want to know how you are. Well, I was fine until I was forced to be trussed and chained!

Everyone thinks I must be "going through hell." When I say that I'm not, that I actually feel lighter and relieved, they can't conceal the disbelief from their voices. But it's true. I'm finally getting out of prison, which is hell.

I know the feeling you spoke of: "That's it, it's all over." It is probably more of a relief for me than it was for you. You were leaving a productive career. I'm leaving a mostly unproductive life of waiting for Godot, the Great Liberator, Death.

Thanks for your prayers. I agree that the prayer switchboard is unattended. Still, sometimes the only way to express our forlorn hope is prayer. Good poetry is a sort of praying, I think, whether pathetic or exultant or whatever.

> Twinkle, twinkle little star.
> Science tells us what we are.
> Nothing but a fusion reactor,
> As science kills the wishful factor.

> —A. Luddite

Sorry, you know I have a split personality reaction to science; marveling at it one minute, fearing it the next. Maybe I just hate growing up.

I hope you enjoy the holidays.

DW

December 27, 2004

Dear DW,

We had a quiet Christmas. Old friends who were going to spend the holiday in Ann Arbor with the family of their youngest daughter invited us to join them. We bought plane tickets to Detroit for December 24th, with return on the 26th, but on the 22nd Zelda came down with a bad cold and a snow storm was closing airports, so I canceled the trip. It was a big disappointment, but as compensation I got the noble role of caretaker and cook. Our Xmas dinner was pork chops with cabbage and a bean salad. Zelda hit bottom on Christmas Eve but the next day began to feel better.

When we visited, you said that you will be transferred back to Michigan City a month or so before the execution. As soon as you are there we will visit. I hesitate to enclose a money order because you may have moved before it gets to Westville. I will anyway.

Is there anything you would like me to do? Please let me know if there is.

With affection,
Charles

6
The Year 2005

13

Last Letters

January 5, 2005

Dear Charles,

Thanks for your letter. No news as of this day. Probably this week they'll set an execution date.

I won't go back to Indiana State Prison until 30 days before my execution. Don't worry about mail, they forward it fairly quickly.

I've been saving *The Brothers Karamazov* for that last 30 days, when I'll need a good long book to read. Right now I'm rereading for the tenth time or so *Thus Spoke Zarathustra*. It's an old favorite. Zarathustra is an interesting character. It's Nietzsche's most popular book by far, but he never knew it. He wrote it in 1883 and published the first three parts to little or no reaction. He went insane in 1889, and part four wasn't published until 1892. I'm thinking that you and he might have shared a lively correspondence if you'd been contemporaries. In *The Antichrist* he argued that the Law of Manu (regarding the caste system) was the sanction of a Natural Order, a lawfulness of the first rank over which no "modern idea" has any power. It does seem to perdure with the consent of Indians. I can't accept such a thing by mere right of birth because genius can spring up even among "untouchables." If he'd argued for a meritocracy I might have joined him on the point of Natural Law, for all men are not created equal. Anyway, Nietzsche is always interesting and thought provoking. I think he was terribly lonely all of his life.

I hope your holidays were happy! I liked annual Christmas letter enclosed with your card. World's going to hell in a hand-basket, isn't it?

As always,
DW

January 10, 2005

Dear Charles,

I received your card and letter today. You said it contained a money order. Usually they stamp on the envelope "Money Order enclosed" and a few days later send a receipt. Maybe they forgot to stamp the envelope.

Nietzsche is misunderstood even today. He would have been horrified by Nazis. They co-opted his concept of the Ubermenschen as a Master Race, meaning themselves. *The Antichrist* is powerful, whether one agrees with his thesis or not. I love *Thus Spoke Zarathrustra* beyond all others. It contains an overview of his entire philosophy.

May you and Zelda be well!

DW

January 14, 2005

Dear DW,

A $50 money order was enclosed with the card. I mention the enclosures because I distrust the people who open and read your mail. I hope you get the money: the Serial Number was 07140882047, the date was 2005–01–05, the Post Office Number 474080.

I bought *The Portable Nietzche* because this was the edition you were reading. As a student I must have read more Nietzsche than I remember because it all seems familiar. I recall feeling the same impatience and irritation then that I experience now reading these texts. Nietzsche pontificates. He is pretentious. I will try to take him seriously. I have more limited tastes than I like to admit.

In the *Encyclopedia of Philosophy* Walter Kaufmann wrote that Nietzsche "reasoned more or less as follows. The only thing that all men want is power, and whatever is wanted is wanted for the sake of power. If something is wanted more than something else, it must represent more power. . . . The acme of power is embodied in the perfectly self-possessed man who has no fear of other men, of himself, or of death and whose simple personality, unaided by any props, changes the lives of those who meet him and even imposes itself on the minds of those who encounter him only at second hand, in literature. . . . Nietzsche's admiration for Julius Caesar bears out our account: it is Caesar's personality and his rarely equaled self-mastery that he found exemplary."

Well, right away this puts me off. People have a lot more in common than "the will to power." Our primate ancestors probably had "pecking orders" in common with many other animals, and this aspect of "the will to power" may have been sustained through millions of years of human evolution. So what? Social bonding, symbolic creativity, and emotional complexity grounded in companionship and love are even more characteristically human. I am put off by the focus on heroic male figures, the "superman" or in Kaufmann's translation, the "overman," even when this is explained as a person who sublimates his passions in a creative manner. It appears stereotypically German and romantic.

One of the most influential social scientists from the 1970s to the present day was Michael Foucault (he died in the '90s). Like Nietzsche, he emphasized motives of power and domination in human affairs. Foucault is interesting, but I don't like his work as much as others do. I will try to overcome my dislike of Nietzsche by reading more.

Yours,
Charles

January 27, 2005

Dear Charles,

I checked on the money order and it was put on my account. They just never gave me a receipt. Thanks.

Still no word on the execution date. I thought perhaps this week they'd set one. Not that I'm in a terrible rush to die, but one would like to have a definite time.

A series of articles was published about me in Evansville. It's based on 25 letters I wrote to a reporter. She doesn't interpret me very well, and she left out all the stuff I thought was better—about our justice system and the death penalty and people. I was disappointed but not mad. It could have been a lot better.

Yes: Nietzsche pontificates and speaks in aphorisms. He's a joy when he hits the other guy but quickly becomes a nasty bugger when he starts humping one of my sacred cows! The game of Nietzsche cannot be played by dismissing his assertions on procedural grounds. You play the game by asking, "What effects or signs would exist in the world if his assertion were true?" If those signs or effects exist you ask whether other causes could explain them as well or better. Many times I deny him and win, but other times I fail and a question lingers in my heart. Either way, Nietzsche makes me think. He makes me look deeper into myself and others than I do without his provocations and assaults upon my sentiments. Nietzsche makes me question and doubt. He makes me laugh out loud. I think he is unique. Love him or despise him, he leads us into a moral quest that we should convene in our lives. If every idea in his head were utterly wrong, he is still a treasure for having this wit and the balls to pick at the question like a scab until it bleeds. I say God bless him. He was often very insightful.

Zarathustra embodies all of Nietzsche's philosophy. He is a wise man and a wise-ass comedian at the same time.

Say hi to Zelda. As always,
DW

February 7, 2005

Dear DW,

I contacted Maureen Hayden at the *Evansville Courier*, and she phoned me soon after. She has two children attending Indiana University and said that she was coming to Bloomington. We invited her to lunch.

From time to time I have thought about preparing a book based on our correspondence but put the idea aside. I suggested at the beginning of our correspondence that you write a book and offered to help as an experienced editor. You were not interested. Later, I thought a book would require research to write chapters to frame our correspondence. I would need to visit your family and other people, study the newspaper coverage of your trial, read the court records, talk to the prosecutors, defense lawyers, and so on. I did not want to do that. Also, I did not see in our correspondence a narrative that would sustain a reader's interest.

Now I think that the hunger strike and the months that followed suggest a narrative line. When we first corresponded and met, you were full of vigor, willful, and trying to persuade Gerald Bivins not to accept execution by giving up his appeals. You persisted with great determination over several years. At the Maximum Control Center you contested the authorities to recover the books they confiscated and to purchase art supplies. Soon, however, the punitive conditions caused you to despair. The hunger strike almost killed you, but it revived your spirits. Finally, the desperate prison situation made you decide not to resist any more.

Despite this narrative thread, I wasn't convinced the correspondence would make a book. Learning about your letters to the *Evansville Courier* changed my mind. The book would begin cold turkey with our first exchange of letters in June 2000. When you described your life and crime in a brilliantly written narrative, I brought up the classic film *Rashomon* to suggest that you consider alternative ways to tell that story. We went on to a sustained argument about human nature, religion, and science.

I would edit your letters without adding anything to the text to "interpret" them. You would speak for yourself in them, and it would be up to the reader to decide what you think, what kind of person you are, and how you have lived. I would edit my letters more drastically, including only enough to maintain the dialogue. I haven't seen the letters you wrote to the *Courier*, but they might be added at the end or in some other way inserted into the narrative of your letters to me. If you agree this would be, like *Notes from Underground*, a first-person narrative.

I will need to edit the letters, but the point is that you would speak for yourself. Narrative thrust would be generated in part by the *Rashomon* effect as new information is introduced about your crime. For example, your first letter did not mention that the victims were tied up and shot in the head. This emerged when I read the Indiana Death Row web site and asked you about it. The fact that you had an accomplice came up later, when you told Zelda and me that your lawyer might get DNA evidence from scraping under Theresa Gilligan's finger nails. Near the end of the book, there might be information about your original defense claiming that you came on the scene after another guy shot the Gilligans, but since Patrick Gilligan was still alive you finished him off.

This development of the story would not be to discredit you. I have not read the newspaper files, except for the first few days after the crime in 1980, and several Maureen Hayden articles. I have not contacted your lawyer or members of your family, or read the court records. The narrative line will come from whatever interest readers find in our exchanges with each other, cutting out irrelevant or redundant material. In this sense, the structure will be the editor's, but the book would be in your voice, describing your life, your crime, your take on the world, and the prison conditions you have suffered. The move of death row from Indiana State Prison to the supermax, and your hunger strike will initiate the denouement. This might benefit with the addition of at least some of your letters to Maureen Hayden, and perhaps other material in the *Courier* files, if you agree.

Do you agree? I am not sure it will work. I haven't reread our correspondence to see, in fact, whether a story is there.

Continued on February 8, 2005

I woke up this morning with a title for the book. Since the denouement involves your reading *Notes from Underground*, the title could be *American Notes from Underground*. Perhaps better, *Notes from Underground: An American Story*. Whatever.

The fact that over the past year you wrote twenty-five letters to a newspaper reporter in Evansville indicates that you want your story told. If that is the case, let me know, and give me your opinion about the proposed reference in the title to Dostoyevsky. Since the novella is famous, it would serve as a framing device to indicate how the book should read.

Continued on February 9, 2005

An e-mail from Jan Pilarski (Saint Mary's College, South Bend) came this morning saying that she visited Michael Lambert, who told her that you were moved to Michigan City yesterday in a van, and that you were "in good spirits and dealing well with things." I mailed this letter yesterday to Westville, but here is a copy to you at the Indiana State Prison.

We can't visit you this weekend, but will head for Michigan City on Tuesday. I envy your ability to enjoy Nietzsche and will try again to read him.

Sincerely,
Charles

February 24, 2005

Dear Charles,

Hi. Thanks for the money order. This will enable me to order one last commissary and to ship some things out.

I've been thinking about our discussion of your letter and book idea. Several friends have proposed books; two of you after seeing the *Courier* "interpretation" of me. I'm really not interested.

I didn't tell my story in letters to the newspaper for myself. That is, I didn't want to be remembered better, or forgiven. I wanted people to know who I had been and how I got that way, and that growth in a positive way is possible even after a terrible start. I hoped that after the news value of those letters waned, that perhaps the psychology or justice and corrections departments of the local university might want them—could draw lessons from them. Other than that I have no interest in being portrayed better. I wanted to leave something for others, not for myself.

Your book idea seems only geared at portraying me in an unfiltered light based upon my letters. When you were here you also mentioned the grossly stilted mitigation report Maureen Hayden sent to you. I feel like I gave society a fair chance to see what went on inside my head. It was others who preferred to show how I looked—psychiatrists, prosecutors, newspaper editors, and writers. I feel like I did my duty and don't want to beat a dead horse (which is not so much a metaphor in this case). So, thanks, but no thanks. I don't want a book about me.

My sister, Kathleen, can give you her address if she desires. It is not mine to give. I do have to correct a misconception. Perhaps it was my poor expression, but it was not because my family was as it was that I didn't give you their addresses. I merely asked why you would want to write people like that? I was comfortable with the status quo, having long since cut my losses, and didn't want that muck stirred up again. Still don't. That was part of the reason, but it was mostly that I did not want to. I'm cursed with a free will.

I should warn you—March 8 and 9 are reserved for visits. My sister and family wants the 8th, and I want the 9th for my spiritual advisor from Oregon, so the 7th is open. Everyone wants to come and spend the same two or three days with me, but this is just impossible. I have to prioritize. I come first—hence the 9th is mine and my spiritual advisor's; Sis comes next, hence the 8th is hers; you and Zelda come next, hence the 7th, and so on.

I feel lighter every day. I had thought that the gravity of things would weigh upon me as I got closer. It is surprising to find levity instead. I want out of prison so bad, and this is the only gate open to me. Plus, it's dignified to have such a solemn ceremonial death. I thank God that I was given the time to reflect on my life and to rectify it as much as possible. I sincerely repent the harm I did others. Therefore, I feel good. I feel at peace. What else could I ask for upon death?

Today is Thursday. Tomorrow I do an interview with an Indianapolis TV station. It will be my only live interview. I'm doing it because I've known the journalist for years and been a pen pal to her. She has never lied to me or tried to elicit anything I didn't volunteer. She has uncommon integrity for a TV journalist. I think that should be rewarded. Her name is Anne Ryder. She works for NBC Channel 13. I hope I do well and make people think.

I was trying to get a loaner typewriter, but it fell through. The warden initially approved my request, but the guy he put in charge of it didn't think the available typewriters were "suitable" for security reasons. I'm in too good a place to quibble about it. I'm just ecstatic that the days of denying me things are over in 13 days. On the 10th I pass beyond the grasp of any human being.

Love to you and Zelda,
DW

Postscript

I DOWNLOADED THE *EVANSVILLE COURIER* ARTICLES THAT DW mentioned in his January 27 letter. The first one compared the suffering of two women affected by his crime, his sister, who was 10 years old at the time, and Diana Harrington, the sister of the murdered woman. It was published on January 14, the 25th anniversary of the Gilligan family murders. This was followed on January 16, 17, 18, and 19 by articles titled "Inside the Killer's Mind," "An Obvious Sociopath," "Playing the Crazy Game," and "Wallace Says He's Changed." They were said to be based on twenty-five letters DW wrote to the author, Maureen Hayden.

DW first wrote to the *Courier* on May 13, 2004, responding to an article by Hayden about his participation in the hunger strike. He volunteered to write at length about himself, answering whatever questions she put to him. He said it would be difficult to remember accurately the person he was when he murdered the Gilligan family, and how, starting from childhood innocence, he became that person. He would try, however, because above all else he wanted his account to be honest. His letters would be a cautionary tale. After his execution, when they would no longer have news value, he wanted the *Courier* to give them to an institution where they could be useful to teachers and others concerned with delinquent youths.

DW's offer was an act of contrition. In a letter similar to one in the present volume, he wrote, "We'd all go mad if we had to live always in raw confrontation with our worst moments," but we are saved by processes of forgetting and the reinterpretation of experience. In this healing process we selectively edit bad memories to maintain a self-image that allows us to get on with our lives.

In the version of redemption DW sent the journalist, he wrote that when the disparity between the self-image and painful reality is extreme and the ability to sustain one's self-image is shattered, "then, like a phoenix, one arises from one's ashes . . . looking around at the wreckage of that old life and beholding the utter desolation of it." But Maureen Hayden, the journalist he corresponded with, was unforgiv-

231

ing. In her view, Donald Wallace had been and continued to be a manipulative sociopath. When we met her she declared that although she was Catholic she wanted him to be executed.

When I learned about DW's letters to the *Courier* I had contacted Maureen Hayden to propose that we edit some of those letters along with mine for book publication. I sent the proposal to DW asking for his approval. When he rejected the idea, I told her that as an anthropologist it would be unethical for me to undertake the project without his consent. In any case, when Zelda and I met her we learned of her intense dislike of DW. This would have made collaboration on a book impossible.

DW had written to Maureen Hayden in good faith, but she hid her contempt from him while encouraging him to continue writing. He later told Sarah Nagy, his lawyer, that Hayden "read everything I wrote as if I had the ulterior motive of justification. . . . I wanted to convey to those on the same path that you can't blame others for your problems. Of all the things I blame myself for, I most blame myself for blaming others. . . . The dawn of my awakening was the day I realized that I was responsible for all my choices. . . . I blame no one but myself. I got a clue to how eisegetically Maureen Hayden was reading my letters when she asked about a simple declarative statement I'd made that I was a deranged 22-year-old dope fiend in 1980. She took this as if I was saying that drugs were an excuse or a justification. So I told her, 'Look, drugs didn't make me do it. . . . I amplified this loud and clear: Mea culpa, mea maxima culpa!" Even so, Hayden summarized the letters to her by writing, "He blames bad parents, bad doctors, bad decisions, bad schools, bad juvenile centers, bad prisons, bad people and a lot of bad dope."

Zelda and I visited DW and argued at length about the present book while he was awaiting execution in Michigan City. I promised to edit our correspondence to maintain his voice, ideas and values, but he was adamant. He had been wounded by the *Courier* articles and would not agree to being "edited" by anyone else ever again. He insisted that one way or another I would "interpret" him, as Hayden and others had done. Besides, he said, two other people were planning to write books about him (later in the argument he said five other people). He didn't want any of them to do it. When I said that royalties should go to an organization opposed to the death penalty, or to his sister, he laughed, declaring that I was trying to bribe him.

After the execution, friends urged me to go ahead with the project. Several were anthropologists familiar with ethical issues in the discipline. Encouraged, I contacted Kathleen Wallace Mason, the sister who was the only family member who truly loved Donald Wallace. Kathleen said that I should edit the letters, and she has approved the finished work, as have Sarah Nagy, his lawyer, and Musa Harry Olsen, his spiritual advisor.

The execution was scheduled for March 10, 2005, just after midnight. Zelda and I planned to join the vigil outside the prison. We told DW we would rather do that than collaborate with the state killing ritual. We arrived from Bloomington in the late afternoon. The parking lot had been cleared, and vans with large broadcast disks on their roofs were parked haphazardly at the end near the prison gate. Local members of the Campaign to End the Death Penalty were unloading tables, signs, and other materials for the protest. Our son, Sam, in sympathy with the cause, came from St. Louis to be our driver. We stayed an hour before leaving to register at a motel. When we returned twenty or so people had gathered for the vigil, but protesters were outnumbered by journalists and photographers. A freezing wind made it difficult to stand outside for more than 20 or 30 minutes before returning to the car to warm up.

The vigil was a desultory affair, even when we gathered to march in a ragged circle near the gate. Zelda gave up a little after 10 p.m. Later four Buddhist monks arrived from Chicago. Large pillows were placed in a row slightly apart from the largely Catholic vigil, and the monks silently arranged themselves there to meditate facing the prison.

Shortly before midnight, guards let the licensed media representatives pass through the prison gate to go where they could observe the arrival of execution witnesses. Our inability to see the witnesses, the late hour, and freezing weather made staying seem pointless, so we returned to the motel. The witnesses included DW's loving sister, Kathleen, who for support was accompanied by her husband and her sister, Shannon. They had spent the day before with DW but persuaded their father not to accompany them, thus avoiding the meeting that DW dreaded. Nevertheless, his father wrote a letter in the *Evansville Courier* saying that God and his church kept him from succumbing to the tragedies in his life. He claimed to love his son, not mentioning that he had abandoned him in childhood and during his years on death row. Finally, with no knowledge of DW's faith, he declared that "Don gave his life over to the Lord Jesus Christ." According to the Bible, he wrote, God would forgive his son.

Other witnesses were Musa Harry Owen, his colleague Baqi Ali, and the Buddhist chaplain at the prison. When DW told us that his spiritual advisor was coming from Oregon, he called him a Gnostic priest. Musa Harry Owen had been a prisoner himself, and from their first exchange of letters DW recognized spiritual kinship with him.

The Indiana Department of Corrections had a rule that no felon can minister to a prisoner during the final hours before execution. Knowing this, Musa Harry Olsen brought with him a letter on departmental stationery from the head of Religious Services of the Oregon Department of Corrections. It was addressed to the Commissioner of the Indiana Department of Corrections and to the Superintendent of the Indiana State Prison. The letter asked that Olsen be allowed to minister to Donald Wallace. Explaining that he had been released from the Oregon prison system 14 years earlier, and since that time had played a positive role in the community, it described his qualifications:

> For a time Mr. Olsen worked closely as an ordained person with the Ecclesia Gnostca Catholica (Thelema), and he is now affiliated with and recognized as an Imam with a Sufi Islamic faith tradition that has its headquarters in the al-Farah mosque in New York. . . . Imam Olsen . . . helps us to conduct religious services in many of our prisons. He is also on contract with the department working as a Community Chaplain in our reentry program for offenders. . . . In both of these capacities Mr. Olsen has been cleared for access to all of our prisons by our superintendents, including our maximum security prison which houses our death row inmates. In 2003, the department selected him from about 1,500 volunteers for the Volunteer of the Year Award. . . . In short, I am writing to endorse Imam Olsen, and to recommend his services to your department. Because of his training and experience, I believe that his presence as the religious counselor or minister for Mr. Wallace will actually add to and not detract from the safety and security you are required to provide for the execution. . . . It is my understanding that your execution procedures allow the condemned man to have one religious counselor with them in the last few hours before their execution. Mr. Wallace has asked for that person to be Imam Olsen. . . . if Imam Olsen cannot serve in that capacity, then Mr. Wallace does not want another chaplain or minister to take his place. In other words, Mr. Wallace will spend his final hours, a time when he is surely in need of spiritual counsel, alone."

The Indiana authorities did not relent.

DW refused any other chaplain and spent the last hours of his life alone waiting to be executed.

Appendix

How This Book Was Made

I HAVE EDITED THIS BOOK AS I SAID I WOULD IN MY FEBRUARY 7, 2005, letter to DW, with the exception that at that time I proposed to collaborate with Maureen Hayden. She had responded generously to the proposal, copying and mailing to me a substantial amount of material about Donald Wallace, including police interviews with Wallace's girlfriend and her sister, as well as the young men who hung out at their house. Hayden also sent a copy of the lengthy mitigation report introduced by the defense when DW was sentenced. In the postscript to this book I have explained that Hayden's dislike of DW made collaboration with her impossible.

This is primarily Wallace's book. I edited his letters less stringently than my own while keeping enough to preserve the flow of our dialogue. When I completed the first year I gave the manuscript to friends, asking them to identify passages that could be further shortened or eliminated, and subsequently after editing each year I sent the growing manuscript to growing list of readers. By the time all five years had been sent out I had enough information to reedit the whole work. It was 429 pages long, a length of 107,000 words. That was much longer than the book I wanted this to be, so I edited a final version of the manuscript, reducing it to 76,000 words.

I am indebted for extensive written comments on the whole manuscript by anthropologists Alan Harwood, Sjaak van der Geest, and Brackette Williams. Others who offered written advice along with insightful discussion of the whole work are Laura Bornholdt, Don Goodman, George Juergens, and Don Lichtenberg. Joyce Adams discussed the manuscript with me, then agreed to reread it to mark passages where deletion would, in her words, make "it more reader friendly." I learned a lot by discussing the work, occasionally at length, with some of these readers, and with Homer Goldberg, Mel Seiden, Robert and Florence Fogelin, Rosamond DuPont, Barbara Butler and Glenn Porter, Lee Mullett, Joy Schweizer, Fran and Truth Schiffhauer, Elizabeth Buck, Henry Swain, Hana Wilson, and Bruce Pearson.

On several occasions Zelda and I discussed the whole enterprise with Donald Wallace's sister Kathleen Mason, and with his lawyer, Sarah Nagy, sending them sections of the manuscript as they were completed, and all correspondence concerned with publication. Musa Harry Olsen, DW's spiritual advisor, approved the book proposal while visiting Bloomington, read the manuscript, and provided the photograph for fig. 12.

Zelda and I read and discussed DW's letters as they arrived and worked on this book together. We believe that capital punishment dishonors American society not only because an innocent person may be executed, but because it forecloses the possibility of forgiveness.

12. Baqi Ali, Donald Wallace, Musa Harry Olsen, March 9, 2005.